3 0063 00364 4434

Fairmount   May 2021

D0906815

be Public Library

FRIENDS
of the
Davenport Public Library

"Celebrate The Printed Word"
Endowment Fund
provided funds for the
purchase of this item

ON THE JOB

DAVENPORT PUBLIC LIBRARY
321 MAIN STREET
DAVENPORT, IOWA 52801-1490

ON THE JOB

The Untold Story of Worker Centers and the New Fight for Wages, Dignity, and Health

CELESTE MONFORTON
AND
JANE M. VON BERGEN

THE
NEW
PRESS

NEW YORK
LONDON

© 2021 by Celeste Monforton and Jane M. Von Bergen
All rights reserved.
No part of this book may be reproduced, in any form, without written permission from the publisher.

Requests for permission to reproduce selections from this book should be made through our website: https://thenewpress.com/contact.

Published in the United States by The New Press, New York, 2021
Distributed by Two Rivers Distribution

ISBN 978-1-62097-501-5 (hc)
ISBN 978-1-62097-663-0 (ebook)
CIP data is available

The New Press publishes books that promote and enrich public discussion and understanding of the issues vital to our democracy and to a more equitable world. These books are made possible by the enthusiasm of our readers; the support of a committed group of donors, large and small; the collaboration of our many partners in the independent media and the not-for-profit sector; booksellers, who often hand-sell New Press books; librarians; and above all by our authors.

www.thenewpress.com

Composition by dix!
This book was set in Garamond Premier Pro
Cover photograph by Jason Cato

Printed in the United States of America

10 9 8 7 6 5 4 3 2 1

CONTENTS

Part V: The Fruits of Their Labors

ON THE JOB

New Labor members pose for a photo after an April 2019 training,
New Brunswick, New Jersey. *Jane M. Von Bergen*

INTRODUCTION:
AWAKENING THE POWER

The International Workers' Day 2020 protest outside a medical supply manufacturing plant on the north side of Chicago wasn't exactly a made-for-television moment. Although news crews did show up at the appointed time, they didn't get the usual footage of workers with arms linked, hands clasped, and banners aloft.

Instead, each protesting worker was standing six feet apart, all isolated icons of determination in the nearly empty parking lot next to an almost-traffic-less roadway.

On May 1, 2020, as the United States and nations around the world staggered under the strain of a coronavirus pandemic, workers' protests took on a different look—masks and separation to slow the contagion. By that day, the COVID-19 virus had already killed 250,000 worldwide, 3.7 million cases had been reported, and the U.S. death toll had exceeded 60,000.

When the pandemic struck the United States suddenly and fiercely in mid-March, many low-wage workers found themselves forced into one of two bad situations. Either they had lost their jobs and faced nearly immediate financial disaster, or else they had kept their jobs, often working in unsafe situations, with the prospect of sickness or death.

Having to choose among bad situations is nothing new for the 60 million Americans who are paid too little for their labor yet fuel a huge share of the economy. They provide the kind of goods and services that allow the rest of us to devote ourselves to career and family. The health and financial crises created by COVID-19 only exacerbated the inequities they already experience.

That's how it felt to the workers demonstrating outside the LSL Healthcare factory in Chicago. But they didn't have to act alone. They were supported by Arise Chicago, one of the country's 225 worker centers. The community labor organization helped the workers draft their demand letter to the company president and present it while news cameras were rolling. The workers who signed the letter—thirty-five in all—were now part of the nationwide worker center movement.

Over the last two decades, worker centers had cultivated enough community trust for workers to know where they could turn for support when the virus struck. The centers could help workers access food or rent assistance, resolve unsafe workplace situations, and, importantly, organize for broader protections such as paid leave.

Making an appeal to an employer for safer jobs and fair pay is a risky proposition under any circumstances. But Arise Chicago and other worker centers across the United States have been helping workers experience the power of collective action. They create a safe space for workers to weigh the risks and to strategize the best approaches to demanding improvements on the job. These community labor organizations provide an environment where community members can learn and develop their organizing and leadership skills.

Worker centers have taken root in small towns, like Morganton, North Carolina; Bryan, Texas, and Graton, California. In some of the biggest U.S. cities, there may be five or ten worker centers, each one with its own personality, mission, and history. Worker centers gather marginalized workers—marginalized because of language, because of immigration status, because their jobs as domestic workers isolate them, or because their employment status is murky as gig or temp agency workers.

Some worker centers have members who work in one industry, such as in poultry production or garment fabrication. Some centers focus exclusively on employment problems; others branch out to assist with immigration issues, finding that they are part and parcel of problems on the job.

What worker centers have in common is a sense of community built through shared experiences—shared experiences on the job, shared experiences on life journeys, or, perhaps, shared experiences adjusting to a new land. What they also have in common is a sense of struggle for higher wages (or any wages), a safer place to work, and a better life.

On the Job: The Untold Story of Worker Centers and the New Fight for Wages, Dignity, and Health focuses on this little-known part of today's labor movement. It's about workers forced to organize for the most basic on-the-job fundamentals: the wages for which they've worked, short rest breaks from labor, and the simple ability to use the bathroom when nature calls.

Worker centers are part of the centuries-long struggle by workers to gain, as the old labor song says, both bread and roses—sustenance and satisfaction. In its simplest form, the labor movement is two or three employees complaining about their boss or their working conditions and then, together, taking some action to improve their situations. On the other end are mass strikes and protests, like the December 2019 pension protest that shut down subways in Paris. In between is what most people think of as "labor"—traditional unions with collective bargaining agreements, officers, budgets, and headquarters.

Somewhere between the two or three people taking on their bosses and the traditional union is what is known as a worker center. Worker centers draw "inspiration from pre-union community-expressions of working people's organizations" such as mutual aid societies or, in Chicago, settlement houses, explained Adam Kader, director of Arise Chicago Worker Center. "And then, interestingly, labor unions are beginning to take inspiration from us."

To illustrate, Kader refers to the "Fight for $15" campaign to support fast-food workers that was organized beginning in 2012 by the Service Employees International Union. "Everything they were doing was from the playbook of worker centers. You might have three out of twenty workers in a McDonald's who would stage a walkout. These are job-placed actions, with community supporters, with a public component, with allies and politicians and media. Labor unions are now looking to worker center tactics for their renewal and their organizing strategies," Kader said.

"We understand the labor movement as encompassing organized unionized workers and unorganized non-union workers," he continued. "You'll hear some young worker center types saying things like 'Unions are old hat and we're the new wave.' We strongly disagree with that. We believe that worker centers are a recent evolution of the labor movement, but the future of the labor movement includes both."

The COVID-19 pandemic, with life and death in the balance, became a crucible for both worker centers and their members. Never were they more challenged, and never were the challenges more urgent. Some worker centers' members are live-in nannies and housekeepers who were fired by their employers, losing homes and jobs in one day. Others are warehouse temp workers, deemed essential, but not essential enough to be provided with protective masks. Some are intimate caregivers in nursing homes or private houses, facing the very real possibility of bringing the virus back to their own families. Others labor in meat and poultry plants, standing just a few feet apart, in danger of contagion.

"Essential" workers lauded as heroes found themselves being called back to work even though exposed to fellow workers who developed COVID-19. Masks weren't available. Hand sanitizer and soap were in short supply. At Arise Chicago, the COVID-19 situation changed, "every day, sometimes hour to hour," said Shelly Ruzicka, the worker center's communications director. "At first it was people losing work, who were financially desperate. But now we've started to hear more and more from people who are still working. A lot of them are essential workers, but whether they are essential or not, a lot of them are working in unsafe conditions. People are scared."

But the anger, if anything, was as contagious as the virus. Around the nation, as worker centers scrambled to help members cope with financial and health emergencies, center leaders began to see and support fresh signs of workers demanding change. "We are hoping that more and more workers will feel their power to organize," Ruzicka said. "It's tragic that it's coming out of extreme necessity to save their own lives. But since that is our current reality, we hope that more workers will do so."

Around the nation, worker centers responded in different ways to the crisis.

The Gig Workers Collective, a virtual worker center representing Instacart grocery and delivery "shoppers," joined forces with groups representing Amazon warehouse workers and people affiliated with Shipt, a delivery service connected to Target, for a job action on May Day 2020. Thousands of them skipped work, said co-founder Vanessa Bain, basing her estimate on the group's seventeen-thousand-member activist list. Many protesters showed up in Staten Island, Los Angeles, Houston, and Richmond, California, to demonstrate. In New York, some posed next to body bags outside Gov. Andrew Cuomo's office, calling on him to do more to protect Amazon workers.

Demand increased for grocery delivery services due to pandemic stay-at-home mandates. In response, Instacart said it wanted to bring on thousands more independent contractors as "shoppers" to meet the crush of orders.

Alyssa Longobardi, a former Instacart "shopper" who now volunteers to handle social media communications for the collective, described the system in place at the time: Instacart put the shopping jobs out for bid, and the worker offering the lowest bid got the order. The system, she said, forced "shoppers" to low-ball each other to get work.

"Especially now, with COVID-19, people are desperate for any source of income," Longobardi said. "Everybody is now low-wage."

Longobardi, who lives outside Philadelphia, had been new to activism, describing herself as a "Goody Two Shoes." "I had never gone to a protest. I never held a sign. I never talked back to my teachers."

The gig workers' struggle was an awakening. "Workers rising up is extremely inspirational," she said. "This makes you feel like you could change something. For me it's reclaiming this voice I didn't know I had."

In Los Angeles, the Pilipino Workers Center responded by renting two houses for workers who need to be in quarantine. Housing is so expensive in Los Angeles that it's not uncommon for a dozen to fifteen low-wage Filipino workers—housekeepers, nannies, and caregivers—to live in one three-bedroom apartment, with two sets of bunk beds per bedroom, plus more in the living room. With COVID-19, the workers' housing arrangements meant it could be as dangerous at home as it was at work if a housemate had been exposed.

"They have to self-isolate, and of course, they are all afraid," said Lolita Lledo, associate director of the center. "If they get sick, where will they go, because they are living in a room where three other caregivers are staying." One member, she said, became sick. His roommates begged him not to return home. First, he lived in his car. Then he set up a tent outside the apartment building. When the Pilipino Workers Center acquired housing, he was one of the first to get a room.

One four-room house, she said, can house four workers who had been advised to self-isolate, while awaiting test results. The other house is for caregivers who have tested positive. "It's a revolving door," she said.

The pandemic "focuses on the importance of worker centers who have grassroots support, because you are one of the groups who are trusted in the community," Lledo said.

It's that same trust and support that Arise Chicago provided to the protesting workers at LSL Healthcare, a company that packages operating room supply kits and other medical equipment. "We are seeing workers organize for the first time because of COVID-19," Ruzicka said. One of LSL Healthcare's workers died from COVID-19. The company didn't inform their employees; co-workers learned it from her spouse, who also works at the plant.

On May Day 2020, the workers stood six feet apart near the front doors of LSL Healthcare. Speaking in Spanish, one read their demand letter addressed to their *padrones*, their bosses. The warehouse, they said, was not properly cleaned, proper distancing was not maintained, hand sanitizer was insufficient, and the lunchroom only has space for three people to eat. They wanted the plant closed for deep-cleaning and they wanted to be paid while they self-quarantined for fourteen days. "Regretfully," they wrote, "you are forcing us to work under unhealthy and possibly dangerous conditions because of the COVID-19 crisis. Therefore, we have decided to walk-out today to protect ourselves, our families and our co-workers. Our health is more valuable than your profits."

While the COVID-19 pandemic brought sickness and death to millions, and crippled nearly every aspect of the U.S. economy, worker centers were more determined than ever to persist and organize. They would be nimble and creative with their tactics. Their work would continue because the virus did not absolve employers of their duty to provide safe workplaces or diminish workers' needs to fight for their rights.

When people are dying, or hungry, or missing wages, or treated with disrespect, worker power isn't their top priority. "No one comes to worker centers because they want to *change* the system," said Martha Ojeda, senior national organizer for Interfaith Worker Justice (IWJ), an organization that mentored many worker centers nationwide.

"They come because they have a need," she said. "Our challenge is how to transform it into an opportunity—to address the need *and* change the system."

For worker centers, Ojeda's insight had never been more on target than during the COVID-19 pandemic. And worker centers rose—and are rising—to the challenge. They are addressing needs and working to change the system. In the fight for dignity and health, they are awakening the power of today's working people.

Arturo Nieto, member, Latino Union, Chicago. *I. George Bilyk*

Jorge Estrada, member, MassCOSH, Boston. *I. George Bilyk*

Part I

Broken Bodies, Broken Hearts

In 2020, the COVID-19 pandemic brought into sharp focus the intersection of worker safety and worker power. Around the nation, the lowest-paid workers found themselves in the highest danger as death tolls mounted. Safety and wages became twin issues, no longer separated into silos of money and health. Both have long been at the core of worker center missions—with worker safety as a key dynamic for organizing and at the heart of campaigns in Texas, California, Massachusetts, and Illinois.

> It's more visceral, because this is my body. This isn't just my financial health; this is my physical health. It's that much deeper.
> —Adam Kader, Arise Chicago

> We just need to stop being afraid.
> —Mirella Nava, Fe y Justicia Worker Center

1

DANGER AND DISRESPECT

When Mirella Nava went to work at an industrial insulation factory in Houston, she didn't intend to become a worker safety advocate. At the time, she didn't know much at all about workers' safety rights, or about the U.S. Occupational Safety and Health Administration (OSHA) for that matter.

What Nava witnessed in the warehouse, where workers cut and prepped insulation to match customer orders, didn't seem right. Dangerous chemicals, but no eyewashes. Overwhelming heat. Broken drinking fountains. No safeguards on cutting machines. Dust everywhere. "It just broke my heart to see things like that," she said.[1]

It would get "hotter than hell" in the warehouse, explained Nava, especially during Houston's sweltering summers. She said the drinking water fountains in the warehouse were broken. Workers often had to bring in their own water and they would get yelled at when they stopped to drink it if they weren't on an official break.

Rock Wool Manufacturing in Houston used a lot of temporary workers—Nava got her office job through a temp agency. They "were sent by the staffing agency and thrown on the line and that was it," Nava said. She never witnessed anyone receiving safety training. The litany of hazardous conditions was long. On more than one occasion, the chemical paint thinner used to clean off industrial glue got into workers' eyes. There was no eyewash station.

Nava remembers the time she brought a worker to the bathroom and helped him wash out his eyes in the sink.

Another time, a worker was looking inside a machine to see why the blades had stopped moving. The door on the machine fell on his head because it didn't have proper latches or locks, Nava said. He wasn't allowed to leave work until he got the machine working again. After he left work, she explained, he saw a doctor to get stitches to seal up the gash. Nava couldn't stand by and say nothing. She spoke with the manager numerous times about the safety problems. "He said he didn't have the money [to make the warehouse safer] and that plenty of people would be happy to do this work."

Speaking up for the workers in the warehouse created a lot of tension between Nava and her manager. Should she risk going over his head?

She did. Nava took the chance to point out some dangerous conditions when officials from the company's Alabama headquarters visited the Houston plant. As they were talking, a forklift caused a pile of boxes hoisted on a pallet to topple to the ground.

Not long after, Nava was fired. Her boss said she was spending too much time going to medical appointments. The appointments were necessary. Nava had injured her hand after falling in the warehouse.

Nava couldn't stop thinking about the workers at Rock Wool she'd left behind. She called her local Univision station to ask for advice. They gave her the phone number for the Fe y Justicia Worker Center (FJWC)—faith and justice worker center. FJWC's office at the time was on the second floor of St. Stephen's Episcopal Church.

Broken hearts, broken bodies—they are all issues that worker centers such as Fe y Justicia encounter regularly. At most centers, including this one, health and safety concerns are rarely what initially compel workers to walk through the door. Most often, they come because they haven't been paid. Often, though, a company that isn't paying its workers is also hurting them in other ways. Health and safety issues become one lever among many—one that grows more important as workers come to realize the gravity of safety on the job.

"It's more visceral, because this is my body. This isn't just my financial health, this is my physical health, this is my mental health," said Adam Kader, director of Arise Chicago Worker Center. "It's that much deeper."

For worker center leaders, health and safety issues serve a variety of functions. They sometimes help to provide funding, through OSHA or academic grants for training. They sometimes act as a membership draw like in Chicago, where both Latino Union and Arise Chicago offered workshops on green cleaning and avoiding harsh chemicals to improve the home environment for domestic workers and their clients. Those trainings can help workers demand the higher wages that go along with increased expertise.

But most important, health and safety issues build worker leadership—the kind of leadership that results in improved safety standards to help workers beyond their own workplaces, or cities, or states. Confronting these issues gives leaders the tools they need to effect change—analysis, strategizing, documentation, communication. They motivate workers like Mirella Nava, who risked everything to make jobs safer for her co-workers.

Nava encouraged some of the workers to join her at the center's Monday-night labor law workshops. "It was a big eye-opener for all of us," she said.

Together, they used bright-colored markers on flip chart paper to map the inside of the warehouse. The "hazard mapping" activity is a familiar technique used at worker centers to dissect health and safety problems. Alejandro Zuniga, the FJWC safety trainer, helped Nava and the other Rock Wool workers sketch the locations of many dangerous conditions. There were cutting machines without safety guards, electrical hazards, and problems with the forklift. The air in the plant was laden with mineral fiber dust from the insulation itself.

"They pointed out all these hazards to us that had previously seemed like normal, everyday things," Nava explained.

Zuniga started volunteering at FJWC in 2010 and has been part of the small staff since 2011. A native of San Luis Potosí, Mexico, he has a kind soul, a generous smile, and abundant enthusiasm for empowering workers to achieve justice. The hazard mapping activity helped the Rock Wool workers recognize something that Zuniga and Martha Ojeda, then FJWC director, see all the time: the power of workers' collective knowledge. Zuniga's and Ojeda's roles involved coaching Rock Wool workers to determine what they wanted to do about the problem. It didn't take long— just a few more get-togethers at the worker center—for them to agree upon a plan.

With the assistance of FJWC, nearly a dozen Rock Wool workers made a formal complaint to OSHA. The worker center's connections ensured that OSHA dispatched a Spanish-speaking inspector to conduct the employee interviews. The results were OSHA citations against both Rock Wool Manufacturing and the staffing agency C&C Personnel, which supplied the temp workers. The firms paid more than $51,000 in penalties for the hazards identified by the workers and confirmed by the OSHA inspector. In a press release announcing the citations, OSHA said: "Any time a worker is exposed to machinery without proper guarding is one more time that worker is in jeopardy of losing a limb or even a life. Failing to adhere to this commonsense safety requirement will not be tolerated." [2]

Joann Figueroa, OSHA's area director in the Houston North office, said she values her staff's relationship with FJWC. "We're able to reach workers we might not have been able to reach in the past." This is particularly true for temp workers like Mirella Nava and the others at Rock Wool. "A temp worker, at times, is not treated or viewed as being the same as a permanent employee in the same workplace," Figueroa noted. However, OSHA's policy is that worker safety is the joint responsibility of the staffing agency and the host employer. "Depending on the circumstances, they [temp workers] could be more vulnerable and potentially not as well trained," she added.

Mirella Nava witnessed this situation firsthand. Her employer's disregard for the law was wrong, and workers were getting hurt because of it. Nava's experience convinced her she wanted to volunteer at FJWC to help other workers. "We need to start speaking up and we need to let the community know that there are centers that exist that will help you and hold your hand step by step," Nava said. "There's nothing wrong with looking for that help or seeking that support."

Some workers are just too vulnerable to stand up by themselves, Nava explained. It makes a "huge difference" when "they're not standing alone."

In her research, Janice R. Fine, the Rutgers University professor and author of the most recognized book about worker centers, found that most workers initially come into contact with a center because they need help recovering unpaid wages or tackling problems with immigration law.[3] It's less often that workers, like Mirella Nava and the others from Rock Wool, will walk through the door because of a safety problem on the job. On the hierarchy of needs, it makes sense. Getting paid to cover rent or buy food is more urgent than safety problems at work.

Dangerous conditions on the job are hugely important, but not at first. "The issues workers come up with themselves, that they self-identify, typically do not include health and safety," said Adam Kader at Arise Chicago. "Disrespect is the number one complaint of workers coming in. With that is usually wage theft. 'I should be paid, and I'm not being paid.' However, the moment we start probing and asking questions, sure enough, there's always a health and safety thing that comes forward."

To workers, he said, it's immediately obvious that they should be paid. And they tend to believe that disrespect is a form of illegal discrimination, although most often it's not, strictly speaking, illegal. It's just unjust. "With health and safety, I think it's more esoteric," he said, before launching into a series of rhetorical questions. "What are the standards that govern the workplace? Do I have a right to a cool temperature in the summertime? Do I have a right to knowing what the ingredients on the spray bottle I'm using to wash this counter are?"

Sometimes, Kader said, workers accept injuries as part of the job. " 'Hey I've always worked in restaurants and I've always had slips. I've always had burns. That's part of the job.' " There's a degree of resignation. "I don't think workers are necessarily apathetic, but sometimes, with some of those details, they don't necessarily see it as an actionable issue," he said. "Until we identify what workers have a right to claim, they might not claim it."

Excessive heat, rickety scaffolds, carbon monoxide, and malfunctioning machinery are the kind of hazards that typically injure workers. On average, 14 U.S. workers are fatally injured on the job every day, and more than 3,100 per day are hurt badly enough that they miss days from work.[4]

The risk of getting injured or being made ill from work is not the same for everyone. An analysis by the North Carolina Occupational Health Surveillance Program reported that Hispanic workers were 1.7 times more likely to die on the job than other workers in the state.[5]

Seven years of data from hospitals in Arizona, California, Florida, New Jersey, and New York found that Latinos were significantly more likely to be hospitalized because of a work-related traumatic injury, including amputations and brain injuries, than non-Latino whites. The rates range from 1.4 times more likely in Florida to 2.3 times more likely in New Jersey. There are also disparities between Black and African American workers compared to non-Latino whites for work-related hospitalizations. Black or African American workers have a significantly higher rate of hospitalizations for machinery-related injuries and assaults on the job.[6]

Jobs in occupations where the chances of being injured or made ill are double the national average tend to be held by low-wage or foreign-born workers, according to researchers with the National Institute for Occupational Safety and Health at the Centers for Disease Control and Prevention.[7] None of this is a surprise to worker centers, particularly those that have been intentional about addressing the occupational health and safety problems in their communities.

At the Workers' Center of Central New York, dairy workers describe the risks of interacting with the animals. One dairy hand witnessed a cow kick a worker in the face, which knocked out the worker's teeth. Cows will push back when workers maneuver around them for milking or when a cow is in heat. At any moment, the fifteen-hundred-pound animal could crush a limb or a body.

Members of Centro de Derechos Laborales in Bryan, Texas, are known for performing skits to illustrate the relentless line speeds at the poultry plant in town. The production line runs as fast as 140 birds per minute. Each worker handles forty-five carcasses per minute, repeatedly twisting, cutting, and pulling the whole birds into chicken parts.

At the Latino Union of Chicago, domestic workers discuss the toll that housecleaning has on their bodies. They move furniture to vacuum and mop. They constantly bend, stretch, and reach. One woman described an employer who insisted her bathroom floor and fixtures be soaked with bleach. The homeowner expected her to work in the space while all that soaking was going on. "That's one of the most horrible stories I heard of," said Analía Rodríguez, executive director of the Latino Union of Chicago. "In every one of our trainings, we have a know-your-rights piece at the end. Then we open up the floor so people can share their experiences."

For too many people, however, hearing about someone getting hurt at work evokes uninformed or blame-the-victim responses: "Accidents happen." "He wouldn't have slipped, if he were paying attention." "She wouldn't have cut herself if she were more careful." "He was stupid for letting the chemical splash onto his face."

Power dynamics between employers and employees are complicated and unequal, and managers are often quick to blame workers. But how could she have been more careful and not get cut? Chicken carcasses were zipping past at 140 per minute. Yes, he was burned by the chemicals, but did his boss give him the supplies needed to do the job safely? Then, too, workers sometimes become resigned to accepting that injuries are just part of the job. Sometimes they blame themselves, saying they should have paid more attention.

A lot of workers don't know their rights. They've lost sight, or perhaps never really understood, that the law requires employers to keep jobs safe. They don't know that employers must provide equipment to do jobs safely. Even workers who know their rights are rightfully afraid to speak up. Raising concerns about safety problems might translate into being shown the door. That's what happened to Mirella Nava at Rock Wool Manufacturing.

The power imbalance in workplaces is exacerbated when workers are desperate for jobs. Immigration status, English competency, skills, and transportation barriers may trap them in unsafe jobs. Workers will take the chance of getting injured rather than the risk of getting fired for raising safety concerns. With at-will employment the norm, it's easy for an employer to sever someone from a job. Chances are slim that a worker would win a retaliation case for raising safety concerns. The odds are even more remote that a refugee or immigrant worker will complain to a boss about unsafe conditions.

"Often, when health and safety issues become very motivating for our members is, unfortunately, after they've had an injury," Adam Kader with Arise Chicago said. "At first, I think there is a lot of self-blame: 'I should have been more careful.'"

There's a difference, though, between someone seeking help after they've been hurt and getting workers to see how workplace safety can be leveraged. "There are some macho guys in construction," Kader explained. "They are complaining about not being paid. They may say they don't care that it's dangerous work. But we can say, after doing this intake, we feel there might be some OSHA violations on the job. They say, 'Yeah, whatever.'

"Well, here's the thing," Kader continued, laying out the dialogue he might use with those workers. "Let us convince you of something. Maybe your prime motivation is the pay. How are we going to get your employer to do that? One angle or pressure point is we can threaten an OSHA violation. Or, maybe there is a reporter covering dangerous construction jobs. That's a pressure point on the employer to get you your pay. Even if you are macho and think you can handle it, use that as a tactic toward getting your goal."

Kader offered another example. "Say you have two workers out of fifty at a plant. They say, 'We're here because we're pissed off about [a wage issue].' We say, 'Let's start something right now. How many other workers can you bring us?'" The workers will describe three other workers, angry about scheduling, plus a few more who must deal with a leak. "Organize them around them being pissed off about the leak," Kader said. "That's a health and safety violation. Now, suddenly, we have fifteen workers. Now, we have a list of grievances. We want to demand all of them. Now we have fifteen people willing to do a job action instead of you two. You two might not be effective or care about that leak but for the people in the other department, it's a constant hazard for them. This is a pragmatic organizing mechanism to get workers to take it more seriously."

It also gets employers to take it more seriously.

"There is a value to having multiple issues to address," said Marcy Goldstein-Gelb, co–executive director at the National Council for Occupational Safety and Health (National COSH). Goldstein-Gelb led the Massachusetts Coalition for Occupational Safety and Health (MassCOSH) when it started the Immigrant Worker Center in Boston.

"Different types of problems have different types of solutions," she said. "You can do a class action suit against an employer. You can go to the attorney general. You can have a potential enforcement situation through OSHA. Each problem may have a different type of tool. People often say a particular agency is weak and that's absolutely true. What you do have is the ability to pull these various tactics together and pressure the employer. You are going to be able to have a range of avenues to take action. We tend to avoid focusing on just wages or just health and safety."

At the Immigrant Worker Center, health and safety has always been central to building worker power. It's that way because of MassCOSH's own history. MassCOSH was founded in 1976 by a small group of progressive advocates from labor, health, and law. They saw and heard how workplace chemicals and dangerous machinery were affecting workers' health and their livelihoods. The advocates also understood the potential for organizing workers to make demands—whether to their own employers or government officials—to address the problem of dangerous workplaces. MassCOSH is one of the oldest of the fifteen COSH groups across the United States.

Because of its expertise in worker safety, MassCOSH is able to support workers in their quest for safer workplaces. And because it has been around for forty-five years, it also understands how to work multiple systems—the courts, the media, and business— to produce results. Goldstein-Gelb gave an example. "In 2006, we had a large group of hotel housekeepers come to us in absolute agony. They could barely move; management had doubled the amount of rooms they would clean in a shift from fifteen to thirty. A couple of them also had bad reactions to chemicals. We did twenty to twenty-five interviews and asked a number of questions," including how many people had to take painkillers just to get through the day.

MassCOSH was able to apply its expertise to analysis of the chemicals involved. "We did a health and safety assessment of the workers and wrote a report," Goldstein-Gelb said.

"The workers were very clear what they wanted to do with the report. They didn't want to bring it to the direct manager. They had already struck out. They had already gone to the manager and it hadn't worked." Again, MassCOSH applied its research expertise to the situation, with staff searching and searching until they unearthed the hotel company's national health and safety director and arranged a conference call. Some of the affected workers were on the call, along with a translator and an ergonomics expert known to MassCOSH. The health and safety manager listened to the call and told the workers they weren't supposed to be cleaning that many rooms. "They didn't want us to release the report publicly," Goldstein-Gelb said. The manager's request didn't surprise her. A week before, housekeepers had rallied outside a different hotel in Boston—ironically, during the American Public Health Association annual meeting. "They probably didn't want that."

The result? Some hotel higher-ups flew into town. "Within a couple of weeks, the workload was cut in half," Goldstein-Gelb said. That's how the centers can build worker power through health and safety campaigns. The question is: What's the end goal? Is it worker power or safer workplaces—or both?

Health and safety training "saves somebody's life, potentially. It happens," said Carmen Martino, co-founder of New Labor, a worker center in New Brunswick, New Jersey, where Martino works as an assistant professor in the Department of Labor Studies and Employment Relations at Rutgers University. "I know a lot of people go to bed at night thinking that's why they do this. There's nothing wrong with that. That's enough for most people who do this work."

But not for Martino. To him, it's a positive side benefit to what matters most—empowering workers to improve conditions on the job. "I saw the potential here is to take education and empowerment, and put them in the same room and add to that so people will come to a different conclusion about what they can and what they can't, what they should or what they shouldn't be doing in their workplace if the workplace is a mess, or where the exploitation is such that, you know, you're getting paid minimum wage, and you're not a human being," Martino said.

"You're just there as a commodity," he said. "I mean, it's all you are. You're a pair of hands, you're a back. You're somebody's path to profit. That's all you are."

In Chicago, Kader agrees. "Our job as organizers is not to deliver the bare minimum for workers," Kader said. "It's to push workers to demand the most they possibly can. Part of this is us informing workers—you can demand more: You can demand gloves. You can demand training on that machine. You can demand a safeguard on that machine. You can demand rests. You can demand longer breaks. It's about helping you expand what workers are demanding."

Through worker centers, workers can demand bread. They can demand roses. And they can demand a safe place to work, as Mirella Nava learned at Fe y Justicia.

"We just need to stop being afraid."

2

OUT OF TRAGEDY, TRIUMPH

The two men were lucky. They managed to grab a balcony railing, escaping the death plunge that killed three other men on their construction crew.

Raudel Ramirez Camacho, twenty-seven, Wilson Joel Irias Cerritos, thirty, and Jesus Angel Lopez Perez, twenty-eight, fell eleven stories to their deaths on June 10, 2009, when part of the platform they were working on detached from the outside of a luxury student high-rise under construction on the University of Texas's Austin campus.

Residents of 21 Rio—with its granite countertops, stainless-steel appliances, and panoramic views of the city—have no reason to know what happened to Camacho, Cerritos, and Perez. There is no plaque or other monument to them or any sign that they were killed at the site just trying to earn a living. But for some Austin residents, the corner of Twenty-First and Rio Grande is notorious. German Zaravia is one of them. He was a construction worker on the project and later became a member of the Austin Workers Defense Project (WDP).

"We risked our lives out there on that worksite," Zaravia said.[1]

One week after the men died, with their bodies barely laid to rest, WDP held a news conference to release a report on Austin's construction industry, *Building Austin, Building Injustice*.[2] The visuals: a collection of worn work boots and a handmade sign, "In Memory of the 142 dead construction workers from 2008 and the three dead LAST WEEK." Detailing low wages, no benefits, and

unsafe conditions, the report's conclusions came as no surprise to
Zaravia and his fellow construction workers.

Writing for the *Austin Chronicle*, Nora Ankrum contrasted
WDP's *Building Austin, Building Injustice* report with Austin's
booming economy:

> The report's most revealing aspect might not have been the data it-
> self, so much as the explicit contrast WDP drew between Austin's
> haves and have-nots—those who were living in the 21 Rios tak-
> ing over the city's skyline and those risking their lives to build
> them. The report was released at a time when most of the country
> was suffering the blows of the recession—yet Austin remained
> relatively insulated. In 2009, it had the second-healthiest housing
> market in the country.[3]

The year 2009 was indeed a notable one in WDP's evolution.
The *Building Austin, Building Injustice* report and the three
worker deaths at 21 Rio were linked. The worker center's research
quantified the labor abuses in Austin's construction industry. The
men's deaths proved the very real consequences. The tragedy was
a defining event, and its aftermath, coupled with the report, elevated WDP's influence. By 2009, WDP had hundreds of members and a dedicated group of volunteer worker leaders. Emily
Timm and Cristina Tzintzún, the center's co-founders, would
make sure WDP capitalized on all of it.

News conferences are the high-profile events that bring attention
to efforts of worker centers like the WDP. But the real work of the
WDP, the work that builds solidarity and power, takes place Tuesday evenings in WDP's office in a sprawling building that looks
like it once housed a construction supply depot.

As usual, the parking lot outside was packed. The dusty lot on
the city's east side was filled with older cars and pickup trucks
parked wherever they could fit. Arriving early meant you might get

a parking spot, but the downside was you'd probably get blocked in. Regulars knew it happened all the time. It was the price for being present where worker power is built in Texas.

Outside, the building's bright blue roof was easily spotted from the road. Inside, staff and volunteers were getting ready for "Workers in Action," the name for the Tuesday-night meetings. It's a community event where WDP members and volunteers educate workers about their rights, assist those who have been victims of wage theft or other labor abuses, and recruit new members.

In a small side room that doubles as the kids' playroom, WDP's workplace justice committee prepared for the main event. Beneath inspirational labor rights posters on the walls and next to children's art supplies, books, and games stuffed on shelves, the worker-led committee discussed the benefits of taking the ten-hour worker safety course offered by OSHA-authorized trainers. The class would make them better able to educate other workers about their job safety rights, as well as help them recognize unsafe conditions and how their bosses should fix them. The class could also help them recruit more workers to attend WDP's safety workshops.

Next on the agenda, the workplace justice committee watched a video enactment of a scenario familiar to many WDP members. A construction site supervisor tells workers to just ignore safety rules and get the job done. He threatens them with deportation. One worker goes to WDP for help, where he learns that regardless of a worker's immigration status, employers are legally required to uphold workplace safety standards. The worker gets help filling out a complaint to the Occupational Safety and Health Administration (OSHA), and the video fades to an image of the Workers Defense Project and its bright blue roof.

Everyone in the room claps, ready for the meeting of the general assembly. Someone starts the rousing chant: "¿Qué queremos? ¡Justicia! ¿Cuándo lo queremos? ¡Ahora!" (What do we want? Justice! When do we want it? Now!)

A visitor and observer at the meeting—even one who doesn't speak Spanish—would feel engulfed in the assembly's spirit of worker justice. It was in the voices, it was in the faces, it was everywhere.[4]

Despite the serious labor injustices they face and the steep uphill battles, the worker members were optimistic and hopeful. They were smiling and laughing. The atmosphere was a testament to the power of mobilization and education. It's the buoyancy that comes from community.

"The Tuesday meetings are the heart, soul, and foundation for all the other work we do," explained Greg Casar, who was WDP's policy director. Casar now serves on Austin's city council—a sign of WDP's growing influence in Austin. Elected in 2014 at age twenty-five, he was the youngest council member in Austin history.

Austin, Texas, has been at or near the top of the list of the fastest-growing U.S. cities. The population of the state's capital and fourth-largest city jumped 20.2 percent, from 790,000 in 2010 to 964,000 in 2018. Technology companies, including Apple, National Instruments, and 3M, have major campuses in the region, referred to by some as "Silicon Hills." Dell and IBM are two of Austin's largest employers. With high-tech employers comes the demand for housing and infrastructure, as well as retail and hospitality offerings. Construction jobs can be good-paying with benefits, but many are not. Working low-wage jobs with no employment security, the people serving the lattes, cleaning the offices, and landscaping around the parking lots weren't experiencing Austin's economic boom.

At Casa Marianella, an Austin shelter for asylum-seeking refugees and other immigrants, case manager Emily Timm couldn't help but notice the growing wealth disparity between the desperate workers coming there and the city's economically privileged. It was equally obvious to Cristina Tzintzún, a senior at the University of Texas and a volunteer with the Central Texas Immigrant Workers Rights Center, a project of the Equal Justice Center, a nonprofit law firm.

The two met and became involved in a joint Casa Marianella and Equal Justice Center project, the fledgling WDP led by Julien Ross. In 2006, WDP became an independent organization with Tzintzún and Timm at the helm. "When we took over, we didn't know how to do anything besides have a lot of passion," Tzintzún told the *Austin Chronicle* in 2012. "We almost failed, too. There were times we didn't pay ourselves. We didn't know if we were going to make it month to month."[5]

Like Tzintzún and Timm, everyone living or working in Austin was experiencing the seismic cultural changes that came with growth. The state capital and home of the University of Texas with its "Keep Austin Weird" vibe and vibrant live music scene was now a magnet for start-ups and technology firms. Many of the immigrant workers who walked through WDP's doors seeking help—primarily with wage theft—were part of Austin's growth story, literally. They were wielding hammers and pouring cement, laborers in Austin's booming commercial and residential construction industry. And they were suffering.

Timm and Tzintzún wanted to validate in a systematic way what they were hearing from construction workers about labor abuses at their jobsites.

Like other worker centers, WDP began with research, collaborating with the Division of Diversity and Community Engagement at the University of Texas to characterize Austin's construction industry. The business community and city leaders touted the industry's role in building the local economy. What had not been studied were conditions for construction workers.

The research team spent a year assembling data from the U.S. Bureau of Labor Statistics, the U.S. Census Bureau, the Texas Workforce Commission, and other public sources. With the help of members and other volunteers, WDP distributed surveys to construction workers. More than three hundred completed the survey. The team also conducted in-depth interviews with seventeen workers and twenty industry leaders.

The research confirmed what Timm and Tzintzún had been hearing every day from construction workers: low wages across the board, no benefits, and unsafe conditions. In early June 2009, the report *Building Austin, Building Injustice* was nearly finished and set to be released. The construction industry was indeed booming, but 64 percent of the workers surveyed had not received basic health and safety training; 45 percent earned wages at or below the federal poverty level; 20 percent had been denied payment for their work. On the job, 41 percent did not get a rest break (other than for lunch) and 27 percent had employers who did not provide water.

As Timm and Tzintzún planned a public event to announce the report, construction projects in Austin peppered the skyline, including the new University of Texas luxury high-rise, 21 Rio. Timm and Tzintzún had no way of knowing that three men would soon die there, becoming the tragic examples of all they were learning.

Six months after the *Building Austin, Building Injustice* news conference with the worn construction boots and the handmade sign noting the deaths of Raudel Ramirez Camacho, Wilson Joel Irias Cerritos, and Jesus Angel Lopez Perez, OSHA issued citations to four of the companies involved in the 21 Rio construction project.

OSHA inspectors found numerous safety violations that contributed to the collapse of the elevated platform: it had not been erected properly, some critical hardware was badly worn, and the platform was being used in ways that far exceeded the manufacturer's design. Zaravia was correct. It was a disaster waiting to happen. OSHA proposed a total of $159,600 in penalties against the firms for safety violations.

On the day OSHA's citations were announced, WDP organized

a vigil at 21 Rio, outside the building that by then housed hundreds of college students. Many of them had left town for the holidays. Fifty workers and their families attended, gathering for a long moment of silence outside the apartment building. For those who know its history, 21 Rio stands on sacred ground. A few workers spoke about the need for safer workplaces. They emphasized that dangerous working conditions are the norm at many construction sites in Austin. It's an injustice.

Someone started a chant: "No mas muertes. Queremos justicia." (No more deaths. We want justice.)

By the time of the vigil in December 2009, WDP had identified eighteen construction workers who hadn't been paid for their work at the 21 Rio project. WDP estimated that a subcontractor based in Florida, Capoera Construction, owed the workers a total of $55,000 in hourly wage plus overtime pay for their final weeks on the job.[6] German Zaravia was one of them.

"No one should have to die for their job," he said. "And no one should have to fight just to be paid."[7]

Perhaps a collective bargaining agreement with health and safety provisions could have helped the workers, but Texas is ranked near the bottom of all states in terms of jobs governed by a collective bargaining agreement.

In 2018, only 5.4 percent of Texas employees were covered by a union contract, compared to 10.5 percent nationwide. Only three states had lower union density. Without the bargaining power of traditional organized labor unions, WDP has become creative in the strategies and tactics it uses to improve conditions for construction workers. One way is going straight to local policymakers.

WDP's survey of three hundred construction workers found plenty of problems. The worker center's demands began with something fundamental: rest breaks. Worker Roberto Garza described his experience: "Well, sometimes you're scared to even get down to drink some water. A couple of years ago . . . we were doing some work at some apartments. [My boss] wouldn't let you get down to drink water and he would just stand there watching you. One time I was fainting because the sun was hitting very hard, and I told him I couldn't take it anymore."[8]

It wouldn't be long before the one-year anniversary of the deaths of Camacho, Cerritos, and Perez. Members of WDP were intent on seeing something positive come about because of that deadly event. They repeated their names. They used every opportunity to emphasize data from the *Building Austin, Building Injustice* report. Their target was the Austin City Council: WDP insisted the city step up to improve the conditions for construction workers.

Success came more quickly than they could have imagined. In mid-June 2010, a year after the three workers died, the city council directed the staff to develop a rest break ordinance applicable to construction companies in preparation for a July vote.

Some industry groups objected, arguing that workplace safety was OSHA's responsibility. They argued that they didn't have enough time to assess the proposed ordinance's economic impact. But momentum was on the side of WDP's worker members.

It didn't hurt that nearly every day in the previous two months temperatures exceeded 90 degrees. At its last meeting in July 2010, the Austin City Council unanimously passed an ordinance requiring employers to provide construction workers with a rest break of at least ten minutes for every four hours worked or face $500 a day in penalties.

The AFL-CIO said the ordinance was precedent-setting. No other state or locality had a law on the books mandating rest breaks for construction workers.[9] WDP had its first new policy victory—and it was a big one.

WDP was not shy about naming the companies responsible for the deaths and labor violations at the 21 Rio construction site.

Publicizing the misdeeds of unscrupulous employers—the ones who violate OSHA regulations, game labor laws by misclassifying their employees as independent contractors, threaten workers who raise safety concerns, or fire workers who get injured on the job—turned out to be an effective tactic to draw attention to the problem.

By 2011, WDP had mastered the tactic of calling out these low-road operators.

The worker center was prepared to use another strategy to improve conditions for construction workers in Austin. It would acknowledge and promote "high-road" companies. They are the employers who pay decent wages, facilitate skills development, offer paid time off and health insurance, and give workers a say in how jobs are done. WDP's Premier Community Builder program would tap into the City of Austin's pledge for green buildings and sustainable development.[10]

WDP wanted the public and decision makers to see "green buildings" as more than efficient energy in the buildings themselves. Sustainability had to also consider the labor of the people who built them.

The Premier Community Builder program was a worker center initiative to certify major new developments as sustainable for workers. That meant making sure construction workers got a fair and livable wage, proper safety training, and were covered by workers' compensation insurance. (Texas is the only state where employers—even in high-hazard industries—are not required to carry workers' compensation insurance.) Developers seeking certification under the Premier Community Builder program had to offer paid time off and hire a percentage of their workforce from local technical schools. WDP pitched and promoted the program as a mechanism to integrate labor practices into Austin's sustainability goals.

In 2012, the city council included the Premier Community

Builder certification components in a deal with the Trammell Crow Company, a Dallas-based real estate developer. The firm was purchasing a 4.4-acre plot of city land to turn into a massive mixed-used development of housing, retail, and offices. "We want to be able to call a building sustainable when it's benefiting the entire community," said Casar, then WDP's business liaison. "If workers aren't being paid and trained properly, that's bad for sustainable development."

Achieving Premier Community Builder certification also meant allowing a WDP representative to monitor the jobsite and speak with workers at least once per pay period. The on-site monitoring was particularly critical because of the layers upon layers of subcontracting on construction projects. It's an environment ripe for finger pointing and averting responsibility for safety hazards or when a worker gets injured. The WDP monitors, peers who could be trusted, came out of the ranks of worker center members. They were trained to identify unsafe conditions.

WDP backed their Premier Community Builder program with research. They teamed up with the Center for Sustainable Development at the University of Texas to answer questions like: How much do Austin residents and visitors care about a business's environmental and labor practices? Do they influence their decisions as consumers?

It turned out people care a lot. Of nearly three hundred surveyed, 43 percent of residents said it was unlikely or very unlikely they would purchase a home if they knew the law had been broken in its construction. Nearly 70 percent of both residents and tourists said they would be willing to pay more rent or a higher hotel room rate for a building that was certified as meeting the Premier Community Builder criteria. The researchers found people linked worker treatment to building quality. They heard comments such as: "I think when you have workers that are given rest and water breaks and receive living wages, appropriate safety equipment, and training . . . I think you get a more respectful product. I think you can see it in the finished product."[11]

The researchers noted that survey respondents would trust an independent monitoring organization over industry self-regulation or regulation by a government agency. Respondents were skeptical of industry groups calling themselves green or sustainable but would give more credence to certifications made by third-party monitors.[12]

WDP's report, *Green Jobs for Downtown Austin*, was released in August 2013. The worker center would use the data to amplify their message about high-road employers. Construction companies that pay decent wages and benefits, while ensuring safe jobsites, could market it, differentiating themselves from the rest.

Significantly, WDP's Premier Community Builder program is no longer voluntary. It is now integrated into city code for major construction projects.[13] It calls for third-party certification, and to date, only WDP is providing the certification, charging a fee to the developer. No other organizations have stepped up to provide the certification.[14]

By 2015, WDP had prepared two more research reports on the experience of workers in the construction industry: *Build a Better Texas*[15] and *Build a Better Nation: A Case for Comprehensive Immigration Reform*.[16] The worker center had evolved from an organization with two paid staffers to one described as a "union in spirit" and "one of the nation's most creative organizations for immigrant workers" by the *New York Times* and its veteran labor reporter, Steven Greenhouse.[17]

A year earlier, the center had branched out from Austin and opened an office in Dallas.[18]

And it was in Dallas where WDP got its second big win—again, tragically due to the death of a construction worker. In July 19, 2015, on a blazing hot Texas day, twenty-five-year-old construction worker Roendy Granillo was installing flooring in an unventilated house in the town of Melissa. That day in Dallas, about forty miles north of Melissa, temperatures nearly hit the 100-degree mark.

That afternoon, Granillo began feeling the effects of extreme heat exposure. He told his supervisor he was feeling ill and needed to rest, but his concerns were ignored, and he was told to go back to work. At about 4 p.m., Granillo collapsed with a heatstroke and was rushed to the hospital, where he died. According to local worker advocates who spoke with Granillo's family, his body temperature had risen to nearly 110 degrees. The heatstroke was so bad that even though Granillo had registered as an organ donor, most of his organs were too heat-damaged to donate.

Diana Ramirez, the campaign manager in WDP's Dallas office who worked with Granillo's parents after his death, noted that Granillo's stomach was empty when he died. He hadn't even been given time to eat that day. "I can only imagine how he must have felt when he asked for help," Ramirez says.

At the time of Granillo's death, his employers weren't required to give him and his co-workers a rest break, even in such extreme temperatures. As of 2020, federal OSHA still doesn't have a specific standard that addresses working in hot environments. Even so, the law requires employers to protect workers from known hazards, including heat. Texas doesn't have a hot environment rule on its books either. Research shows that workers are at the highest risk of heat-related death when not given enough time to acclimate to hot working conditions.

WDP first proposed the Dallas rest break ordinance in June 2014. They modeled it after the ordinance passed in Austin in 2010.

By now, WDP had more than ten years of policy experience under its belt. It also could mobilize workers to show up at city council meetings and it had a reputation for not backing down in a fight for safety and economic justice. But because of WDP's effectiveness, the business community had prepped its allies on the Dallas City Council.

Ramirez and Bethany Boggess Alcauter, WDP's research coordinator, remembered the litany of arguments against a rest break ordinance. Opponents said that it doesn't get that hot in Dallas, or that regulating rest breaks was OSHA's responsibility, or that there weren't enough heat-related deaths to warrant such action. A council member wondered aloud why Latino construction workers would need a rest break at all after having traveled through the desert just to get to the United States.

"Some of the comments were just racist," Ramirez said. "We were a bit prepared to hear something like that in a one-on-one meeting, but it definitely surprised me to hear this said at a public hearing."

At one point, Alcauter said, policymakers offered up an alternate ordinance that focused entirely on educating construction workers about heat stress without actually mandating a rest break. WDP rejected the alternative and continued pushing for an ordinance with teeth.

Then, on July 19, 2015, Roendy Granillo died from heatstroke.

It marked a turning point in WDP's mobilization in Dallas. Like they did after the three workers fell to their deaths in Austin in 2009, WDP leaders made sure that Granillo's death would force lawmakers to act.

Sixty days after Granillo's funeral, WDP organized a "thirst strike" demonstration outside of the Dallas City Hall building. Their demand was an ordinance requiring rest breaks for construction workers. Gustavo Granillo, Roendy's father, made personal appeals to the city council. His son's death could have been prevented. Don't let another construction worker die this way, he pleaded.

In December 2015, the city council took up the measure. It mirrored the ordinance in Austin: a ten-minute rest break for every four hours of work. It passed, 10–5.

"On the day of the vote, it really was amazing," Ramirez said. "Roendy's parents were there, our members were there . . . the whole room started clapping. It was a long fight and people were tired, but it reenergized everyone to know that if we keep working hard, things will get better. Now, workers in Dallas feel like they have a voice."

3

BODY, MIND, HEALTH

Kathy Ahoy stood with her hands propped on the bed of the small pickup truck. She was ready at any moment to grab a plum—or a condom—and offer it to a day laborer. As the *jornaleros* gathered in a parking lot in Oakland, California, she looked content in the background, wearing a baseball cap and jeans. Nearby, Gabriela "Gabby" Galicia and Francisco Matias, two leaders of the Street Level Health Project, handed out pint-sized takeout food containers with warm scrambled eggs over seasoned rice to the large group of *jornaleros* assembling there, at the Home Depot.

On any given day in Oakland, and depending on the season, there are two hundred to three hundred day laborers who gather in parking lots or on street corners. They are part of an underground economy in California that leaves $8.5 billion in various state taxes uncollected each year, according to government estimates.[1] In Oakland, *jornaleros* wait in hopes of being hired for a painting or carpentry job, a landscaping or roofing project, or to work on a moving crew. At just one Home Depot—the one in Oakland's Fruitvale neighborhood—there can be as many as eighty *jornaleros* waiting to be hired to labor for a day or two.

Although a founder of Street Level Health Project, Kathy Ahoy's practice of staying out of the limelight is why Street Level has evolved. She has been successful at encouraging new leadership. "She deeply cares about the community," said Galicia, Street Level's executive director. "She knows that young people are open

to trying new things and different solutions." Whether at the
helm or on the sidelines, Ahoy maintains her singular focus on
health—no matter how that manifests itself with Oakland's underground workforce.

Ahoy worked as a public health nurse in Alameda County. In
Oakland, she witnessed how the crack (cocaine) epidemic in the
1980s destroyed lives and neighborhoods. As a nurse, she grasps
the ways that well-being is shaped by poverty, jobs, housing, and
racism. And, that's why she also seeks social change. Working for a
government agency, however, limited her ability to effect the radi-
cal change needed to build a community healthy in both mind
and body.

So Ahoy decided to address community health needs in a different way. She started Street Level Health Project in Oakland's
Fruitvale area in 2000 with a group of volunteer healthcare providers. It began on the corners, by talking with day laborers about
their healthcare needs. One of Street Level's early partners was
the occupational health clinic at the University of California,
San Francisco. Its director, Bob Harrison, M.D., recruited medical students to survey Oakland's day laborers about their health
needs. What they heard, however, was not about healthcare. The
day laborers talked about needing more work, about getting better, safer jobs, and wanting classes to learn English—issues at the
heart of income and security that are obstacles to well-being.

Kathy Ahoy and the other volunteers' expertise were in nursing
and medicine. They stuck with what they knew and provided basic healthcare, but they also identified services in the community
to help day laborers with other issues. It is why Street Level Health
Project's largest program isn't strictly limited to health in the traditional sense.

That's also why they created the Oakland Workers' Collective
(OWC), which they see as a natural extension of their health-
focused efforts.

OWC's programs address workers' needs to know their rights,

get training, build camaraderie, and confront exploitation, such as wage theft. The other Street Level programs complement OWC's with weekly offerings of mental health consultations, nutrition counseling, health insurance enrollment assistance, fresh fruit and vegetable distribution, and medical services. Body, mind, work.

These days, Ahoy says she's retired and no longer has a formal position with Street Level. But every Monday, she accompanies the outreach team to the ten or so spots where *jornaleros* assemble in Oakland. She brings her bag of supplies packed with bandages, antibiotic cream, cleansing wipes, condoms, and other tools of the trade for a public health nurse.

Ahoy doesn't speak much Spanish, or Mam, the Mayan language of Guatemala. Her calm, kind nature puts people at ease, so over the years, she's found a way to communicate with day laborers. It's the simple things, like noticing an injured finger wrapped in a soiled bandage. She motions she can fix it. Or she gestures toward a rash on a laborer's arm, as if to say, "May I look at that for you?" Of course, with the Spanish and Mam speakers on the outreach team, a person to help with translation is never too far away.

On the corners, Ahoy sees familiar faces. She looks out for ones she brought to the clinic or those she knows are diabetic. She keeps a lookout list for follow-ups. She also notices new faces. They often appear young and strong, but their eyes and demeanor show pain. Ahoy will tell you that there's a lot trauma in this community. Some of the *jornaleros* may have just arrived in the United States. They are away from their families, they don't speak English, they may not have a place to stay; they want to find work, but fear being arrested.

However troubling their lives in Oakland, the *jornaleros* may be also suffering because of something they escaped. It's an experience that's personal to Ahoy. She was a refugee, too.

Following a border dispute in the 1950s, nationalist policies in India led to the imprisonment of thousands of the country's ethnic Chinese people. Kathy Ahoy's family was interned in India for three and a half years. Part of that time she was sponsored by the Loreto Sisters of Calcutta. Along with her classmates, she was required to help Mother Teresa's Missionaries of Charity with their service to the poor. Outside the school property, the students would bring food to the poor and distribute medication to people suffering from Hansen's disease, also known as leprosy. When Kathy Ahoy came to the United States as a refugee, she brought her kindness and hunger for justice.

Mario Pina first walked through the doors at the Street Level Health Project in 2005. "I was walking in the neighborhood and saw the sign and I decided to walk in. I needed some medical care. The doctor was able to provide service in my language." With a chuckle, Pina added, speaking in Spanish as Galicia translated, "Although he was an American white, he spoke Spanish sometimes better than me."

The physician he remembered was Andrew Herring. With Kathy Ahoy, Herring co-founded Street Level Health Project. The free clinic provided primary care services, largely to recent immigrants who settled in Oakland. At its original location, the clinic shared a small space with service organizations that were helping neighborhood residents with other basic needs, such as housing, clothing and personal care products, food, and public transportation.

From the start, Herring and Ahoy's vision for the Street Level Health Project was community-based, meaning a person's health is influenced by social, economic, and environmental factors. Well-being depends on employment, safe housing, nutrition, and a social network. Building out Street Level's programs required listening to the community and asking about their needs.

"One of the reasons the food program started was because a lot of the day laborers would come to the clinic complaining about headaches and stomach aches," explained Galicia, Street Level's executive director. "You're waiting on the street, maybe you don't have a steady job, you don't make a lot of money, so of course it would be hard to find a way to eat," she said.

Street Level partnered with Oakland Catholic Worker to provide a simple meal of rice and beans. "Those were the first meals we offered to the community. We could put it together easily and it would bring workers together," Galicia explained. "They could have conversation and also sustenance."

Street Level's food program, coordinated by Maria Rios, now feeds thousands of people each year. It was Rios who prepared and carefully packaged each container of *huevos y arroz* or other breakfast offerings brought three times per week to day laborers on the corners. She's the master of Street Level's compact kitchen, also cooking meals for the Monday lunch program and the supper that precedes the OWC's workers meeting each week. Rios also manages the Thursday community distribution of produce and other food.

Rios first connected with Street Level when she needed medical care. She started volunteering with the food program and soon was managing it. "It's fulfilling to be able to help people in need, just as happened to me when I needed it," she said. "Filling people's stomachs is only part of the work. More than anything, it is the moral support that they leave with. We are all family and we try to make the community feel this way."

Street Level's relationship with the Alameda County Food Bank, along with Rios's talent in the kitchen, nourishes each plate. Before one week's OWC meeting, twenty members enjoyed stewed chicken, corn on the cob, and a plum and apple salad.

"What we hear from workers is they eat whatever is the cheapest. It's fast food or something from the Dollar Tree that is microwavable. A lot of them might not have access to a kitchen or a place to cook," Galicia explained. "I think this is what's unique about our center. We are talking about the whole person, all of the things that affect them. How not having a sustainable job or a long-term job affects all of these social determinants of health."

Mario Pina had a stable landscaping job for fifteen years. He worked for a large firm that had contracts all around Oakland. So he wasn't working as a day laborer when he walked through Street Level's door for the first time. He needed medical care but was seeking more than that.

"We leave our countries behind. We leave our families and our communities behind. One of the things that is really needed, and what I was looking for, was to build community," Pina explained. "I was looking for people just like me who would understand what I was dealing with. That's what the organization has provided for a very long time."

Pina has been an active member of OWC since 2005. He attends the collective's weekly meeting and the other programs and events. From time to time on a weekend he might take a job from the center's job line, which connects members with employers. But for Pina, most important was belonging to a community.

In 2017, Pina was laid off by the landscaping company. "I didn't feel the impact completely because I knew I had the Oakland Workers' Collective to fall back on." He refers to the community as a family.

The OWC comprises mostly day laborers, *jornaleros*, but that's too simple a definition. It is a community of immigrants in Oakland, with some being new arrivals and others residents for decades. Many speak Spanish, but some speak Cantonese, Nepali, and Mam. The community includes young men who left wives and young children behind, while others have children born in the United States. There is talent galore—poets, street theater performers, musicians, and muralists who paint images of celebration and struggle.

Artwork created by OWC members was on exhibit at Oakland's Peralta Hacienda Historical Park. *Undocumented Heart: Oakland Day Laborers Tell Their Stories* is an indoor and outdoor exhibition that was the culmination of a yearlong project for the day laborers. They were guided by the expertise of three artists specializing in textiles, painting, and graphic design.

Pina was one of the thirteen members telling stories of migration and resilience through artwork. Pina's singular reason for coming to the United States for work was to ensure that his sons and daughters received an education.

"The only people in Mexico who have access to higher education are people who are rich," Pina explained. "I had to come here so they could to go to school to be professionals." He is a humble man, but he speaks with great pride about his children. "I have given them a tool for life—an education—that no one can take away. That was my hope and dream for coming to this country."

Meanwhile, though, there was work to be done.

Street Level's doors opened, as on most days, at 9 a.m., with folding chairs arranged in rows like a waiting room. Only a few minutes passed before staff and volunteers were engaged in one-on-one conversations with people who had come through the door. One staffer was talking with a man to explain how OWC's job line works. A medical student was signing in mothers and children to see the doctor. A health navigator from Alameda County was at a desk helping people enroll in one of the state's or county's health insurance programs.

A petite woman tapped Francisco Matias's arm, motioning him to a more private spot in the room for a conversation. People in the community who speak Mam know Matias. They seek him out. They trust him.

"Many healthcare and social service organizations speak Spanish and English, but not Mam," Matias said in Spanish, speaking through a translator. "They come here because they are more comfortable speaking their own language." Matias began volunteering at Street Level as a translator for the health clinic. It wasn't that he had extra time on his hands. He worked nights at Walmart stocking shelves and as a day laborer in construction and land-scaping. "I knew about Street Level's services, and at that time, when I was waiting at the corners, there were other people who spoke Mam like me. I naturally started stepping in and letting them know about the program here," he explained. "One day I was using the lunch service, and the executive director and the manager of the clinic approached me about an opportunity to work part-time for the organization." That was nearly ten years ago.

"We have been a team for a very long time," Galicia interjected. "I was the outreach coordinator. I speak Spanish, but I didn't speak Mam. We needed Francisco to connect with the Mam community."

"Recently, a lot of people are looking for their detained family members," Matias said. "They don't know what happened to them." Matias knows the system to help them get answers, a useful ability given the Trump administration's hostility to immigrants. "With everything that is happening, he has a lot of experience with this," Galicia explained. "He knows the questions to ask and where to find the information."

Matias said he "loves talking to people" but his approach means he does a lot of listening.

OWC functions the same way. Once a year, about twenty OWC members organize a retreat. They set priorities for the topics of their weekly meetings, such as training on specific workplace hazards, vocational skills development, and health and wellness concerns. They discuss getting involved in local or state campaigns on policies that affect the rights of workers and immigrants. They think about different events to participate in during the coming year and how involvement in all these activities will advance safe and dignified employment for workers who are at risk of exploitation.

"We come back to the office after the retreat and we figure out who our partners are in the community" to pursue this work, Galicia said. "It has been a great experience bringing all these partners in. On the one hand, we learn from them and on the other hand, they learn from us."

Galicia started with Street Level in 2010 after graduating from University of California, Berkeley. She was hired to do outreach, specifically to make day laborers aware of Street Level's healthcare services and food programs. At first, Ahoy instructed her to sit down during the week's lunch program and just converse with people.

Then, Ahoy added another layer to Galicia's orientation.

"Kathy Ahoy took me out to the street to give flu shots. I wondered, 'What? We just show up?'" Galicia recalled. "Kathy said, 'This is how we do outreach at Street Level.' She handed me some flyers about the organization and told me to just talk to people while they're standing there."

Ahoy and Galicia listened carefully to the *jornaleros* they served on the corners. They learned and built programs to match.

For example, they learned about wage theft, and developed OWC's hiring hall and job line to address it. Day laborers are vulnerable to exploitation because of their immigration status, language barriers, and uncertainty about their labor rights. OWC's job line is designed to address some of the abuses experienced by *jornaleros*.

A business or homeowner uses an online form to make a request to hire workers for construction, landscaping, moving, housecleaning, and other jobs. OWC asks each potential employer to provide details about the job, including photos of the project. OWC will identify the next worker in the queue who has the expertise for the job and make the match. Employers who have used the job line before will often request workers by name.

Employers commit to pay the collective's hourly wage that, in 2019, started at $17 per hour, a few dollars above Oakland's 2019 minimum wage of $13.89. Employers are required to pay workers in cash each day, regardless of how long the project lasts. The worker keeps 100 percent of the pay. Neither the employer nor the worker is charged a fee for OWC's job matching service. Employers sign a contract and are expected to comply with all federal and state labor laws. This includes the California law that requires a homeowner's insurance policy to provide workers compensation coverage for "residential employees."

Getting paid in cash addresses the problem of bounced checks. Reminding employers about workers' compensation insurance ensures injured workers aren't out of pocket for medical care costs. Receiving details about the job assignment guards against a worker showing up for a job that is laden with hazards or wildly different than expected. OWC's job line demonstrates that a process developed by day laborers can safeguard against these types of exploitation.

OWC also partners with Centro Legal de la Raza to provide low-wage workers with legal services, particularly to address wage theft, unsafe conditions, and workplace injuries. "It wasn't until the lawyers started coming to the streets with us," that the *jornaleros* knew they could turn to them for help, Matias said. Now, once a month, there'll be an on-the-street workers' rights training, followed by an invitation to come to the office that day for legal help.

Matias said he always encourages day laborers to come to the center. Talking about shared experiences can be empowering. "We say, 'Come. Come and talk with us.'

"Now everyone's hearing it and they say, 'Oh that's happened to me, too' and another, 'Me, too. Maybe we want to do something,'" Matias said.

"It's really about building the community," Galicia added. "They get to see familiar faces, at least once a week," referring to OWC's Tuesday meetings. "They know this is a safe space. It's a common place with this group of people coming together. It comes up in conversation that [the collective] is family."

Building a community of day laborers is challenging. On the corners, the men compete for a limited number of jobs. They are used to working on their own, calling their own shots. There are jobs where they work with other day laborers, but when they get back to the corner, they don't usually think of those men as co-workers.

But even on the corner, Street Level is trying to build community. In June 2019, the community issue revolved around the Home Depot parking lot—the same lot where the Street Level team distributes bandages and breakfast from the back of a pickup. Located on Alameda Avenue near I-880 on the far west side of Oakland, the Home Depot lot has been one of the best-known spots for contractors and homeowners to hire day laborers.

As informal as the arrangements were—no paperwork—there was an accepted protocol for how business was conducted in the parking lot. But tensions had been mounting as day laborers became caught up in Oakland's housing crisis.

An aged metal fence lined the Home Depot parking lot. On the other side was a large encampment where some of Oakland's four thousand homeless residents were living. Tents and tarps packed the dusty area. Jeans and T-shirts hung on makeshift clotheslines. RVs and cars served as shelters. Shopping carts were piled with people's belongings. Large holes had been cut in the fence so people could climb through.

Home Depot and its customers didn't like being approached in the parking lot by the homeless. Home Depot was paying city police overtime to patrol the parking lot. Pressure from Home Depot, residents, and housing advocates was near its boiling point. The *jornaleros* were also upset. This had been their preferred spot to get jobs, but the police and Home Depot were limiting them to smaller and smaller areas in the parking lot.

Galicia heard their frustration, even as she explained that Home Depot owns the lot and has the right to control it. Galicia and Matias conversed with the day laborers like a tag team. Their responses floated back and forth, hers in Spanish, his in Mam. Something was going to happen with that parking lot, and they wanted to make sure the *jornaleros* were part of the conversation. "What do you guys want?" they asked again and again.

There was no easy answer. However, several months later Oakland closed the homeless encampment, with the effect of resolving the situation for the *jornaleros*. It was back to business as usual in the parking lot.

Maybe negotiating this kind of issue wasn't what Kathy Ahoy had in mind when she first started checking blood pressure and bandaging wounds for the *jornaleros*. But that's the point. Street Level Health Project subscribes to a broader definition of health. If the workers couldn't get jobs, they wouldn't be able to afford even the most fundamental elements of health—food, shelter, and security.

As the situation shifted in the Home Depot parking lot, one thing remained the same: there would always be friendship, flu shots, bandages, safety training, eggs, rice, and a big bottle of sriracha sauce dispensed from the back of a pickup. Body, mind, health.

4

SAFE SPACE, OPEN HEARTS

Outside, a steady rain soaked the streets of East Boston, an immigrant neighborhood so new to gentrification that Spanish *mercados* have yet to give way to cafés selling lattes and craft beers.

On the windows of the East Boston Neighborhood Health Center's Education & Training Institute, the rain coursed down the panes like tears. Inside, wearing a shirt that said "No Bad Day in Aruba," a woman was crying. Of course, East Boston isn't Aruba.

And truthfully, Saturday wasn't a bad day for the woman, either. In some ways, it was a relief. There, in a room filled with fifteen immigrants, she could tell her story. Milagros Barreto, organizer for the Immigrant Worker Center, put her arms around the woman, offering comfort and Kleenex. No name for this woman, she was too ashamed.

At that moment, Barreto's work wasn't about job safety or wage theft or the economy or any of the other important issues that draw people to trainings held by the Immigrant Worker Center, a project of the Massachusetts Coalition of Occupational Safety and Health, known as MassCOSH.

"This space opens her heart," Barreto said. "It opens hearts and minds."

On the agenda for the Immigrant Worker Center that day was a session of the center's Leadership Institute.

To lead, knowledge matters, so on that rainy Saturday, the knowledge was in the form of economic training from Riahl

O'Malley, director of education for United for a Fair Economy, a national grassroots group based in Boston that challenges the concentration of wealth and power, working toward a resilient, sustainable, and equitable economy.

Other sessions focus on media training, advocacy, the political process, and group dynamics, as well as the laws and regulations involving wages, safety, sexual harassment, discrimination, and, so important these days, retaliation. Bringing the workers together for the August 2018 meeting was longtime MassCOSH organizer Erika Sanchez. Sanchez first came to MassCOSH seeking help for a community member. That led to volunteering, and eventually she joined the staff.

"She's a leader in her community," Barreto said.

Lots of organizations talk about worker empowerment and leadership, but MassCOSH takes it a step further, and makes it part of the deal, in return for services rendered. "We don't just want to provide you with an attorney and then say goodbye," said Jodi Sugerman-Brozan, executive director of MassCOSH. "We want workers to commit to staying connected."

Through MassCOSH, the Immigrant Worker Center has connections with lawyers who will help with workers' compensation and wage theft issues. In Massachusetts, a worker's immigration status is irrelevant when it comes to receiving medical care and lost wages because of a work-related injury. Employers are required to carry workers' compensation insurance, and when they don't, MassCOSH's partner lawyers can help workers get the legal and medical help they need, plus fight off any retaliation attempts.

What does the center want in return?

"They have to commit to coming to regular meetings. They have to be trained and become trainers. They have to provide peer support. That's incredibly valuable. They have to become leaders and activists," Sugerman-Brozan said. "They support each other. 'Here's what happened to me. Here's a doctor I really like,' so that generally, they aren't feeling so alone."

They are expected to recruit members from their social circles, workplaces, and churches. If there's a hearing, a handful are required to show up, wearing MassCOSH T-shirts, to show the judge and lawyers that the injured worker has people in his court who understand the law. And they have to agree to donate 1 percent, up to $500, of whatever financial settlement is achieved back to the worker center.

All of this isn't simply bullet points on a website. To get the help, the workers have to sign an agreement, showing that both sides are serious.

"We are focused on building the leadership of workers and empowering them," she said.

MassCOSH, part of a national network of fifteen COSH groups, sees the development of worker leadership as key to its mission of creating safer workplaces by aligning expertise in labor, health, and law. Because of its expertise in occupational safety, MassCOSH is able to support workers in their quest for safer workplaces.

On Saturday, speaking in careful Spanish, O'Malley distributed a package of charts showing income distribution in the United States by gender and race, the number of deportations, programs that lead to middle-class lifestyles—the GI Bill, Social Security—and those that block it, including immigration quotas and redlining.

But for his first question, he asked the group to divide into pairs and tell each other how the economy is doing where they live and work. Later they were invited to share their immigration stories, again in pairs. This was the one that drew tears.

Wiping her eyes, the woman said she had never learned to read and write. As a young girl growing up in El Salvador, she was sexually abused, with her abuser telling her that if she told anyone, he'd kill her father and her mother. Eventually, she escaped to the United States, carrying her shame with her, unwanted baggage.

"Because I don't know how to read and how to write, I have

to do the worse jobs," Barreto said, relaying the words from the woman, who was probably in her mid-fifties. Her lack of literacy, coupled with her lack of documentation, made her more vulnerable than most. That's why the education she'd gain that day, one PowerPoint slide at a time, would make a real difference—and maybe even make it a good day.

Getting the coffee ready for the leadership training in East Boston, Barreto talked about why the economics lesson is so important. "Our goal is to go deeper into different topics, why we do rallies. It creates an understanding."

The real understanding begins when a worker is injured or isn't paid. Before that, Barreto said, they stay focused on working. "They come here from another country with a goal, to send money home. They don't have time for workers' rights. People are just dedicated to work, work, work, just to earn money."

Often, they are working two and three jobs, to the point that it takes a toll on their bodies, she said. Injury is almost inevitable. Then, unable to work, at least for a time, they start new lives as advocates.

Jorge Estrada's new life of advocacy began several years ago when he hurt his back lifting a hundred-pound bag of potatoes at the restaurant where he worked. He went to the hospital, and got a doctor's excuse for missing two days of work. When Estrada returned to work, he noticed he didn't get paid for those days. When he raised the question, the boss said he didn't pay sick time.

Estrada, who came from Mexico in 1975, found out about the Immigrant Worker Center and MassCOSH from someone handing out leaflets at a train station. He called, he got help, and now he's active, campaigning at the state house for measures to stop wage theft. "I'm not very smart," he said, "but I'm learning. I used to be very shy."

Estrada, in his sixties, now works at a different restaurant, where he's treated well. The owners like his work ethic, and Estrada believes they respect him because he stands up for his rights on the job and encourages his co-workers to do the same.

"The owner saw me on TV protesting," Estrada said, "and he saw that I know my rights. I think they respect me more."

From where Estrada was sitting, he could look across the room at Hugo Perez, in his forties, who, until he was injured in June 2018, flipped burgers and boiled pasta at a restaurant in Boston, sending money home to his family in Colombia.

Then, one day, Perez nearly fell off a step in the kitchen. He came down hard on his knee, which swelled. The head chef tried to convince him that a little rest would fix it, but eventually Perez went to the hospital.

There was no sick pay from the restaurant.

These days, his knee is improving, and the center found him a lawyer to help with workers' compensation. And, because of the agreement with the center, Perez is attending the sessions, although, he says, emotionally he's not strong enough to be a leader. "The financial situation is affecting me a lot," he said. "When you stop getting money and you stop giving money, you feel like a loser."

Mirna Santizo hasn't returned to work yet either.

Santizo came to the United States from Guatemala more than a decade ago. Eventually she got work in a recycling company, separating soda cans and plastic soap containers from the line of trash passing before her. The work was hard, the pace fast, and the humidity made it almost unbearable.

Then one day at work about two years ago, "I started to feel a pain in my head. I started feeling dizzy, like I was going to fall. I was chewing gum and the gum fell out of my mouth, because my face turned to one side," she said through a translator.

Hospitalized with a stroke, Santizo, in her sixties, got a lawyer to help her. But the lawyer did little, and Santizo's problems were compounded by translation issues. She was injured by a "*derrame cerebral*," a cerebral hemorrhage. Somehow in translation, the lawyer thought it was "*rama*," that a branch had fallen on Santizo's head.

The worker center found her a new lawyer, who is attempting to untangle the mess. Meanwhile, Santizo, leaning on a cane, regularly attends the worker center meetings.

Santizo no longer works at the recycling plant, but she keeps in touch with her co-workers. "Three people in the last month have fainted there because of the heat," she said. "I talk to them, but they are afraid, because they think they are going to be fired."

Barreto shakes her head. Yes, it's a different time now. Yes, President Trump has come out tough against immigrants, but, even with that, she asks rhetorically, "What has changed?"

"Yes, it's super hard and people are in the shade, afraid to come out," Barreto said. "But you still have the right to go to OSHA. You still can file retaliation claims. You can still go to court. The rights are still there."

"That's why we still need the worker centers."

5

HE COULDN'T MAKE HIMSELF BEG

No matter how desperate he was, Arturo Nieto couldn't bring himself to do it. He couldn't bring himself to chase the trucks as they pulled up to Chicago corners to find the Mexican day laborers waiting for work. He couldn't make himself beg.

It was, he said, humiliating. He still had his pride, if little else. "You have to fight to get the work," he said. *"Pick me. Pick me."*

"It's kind of rough," he said. The men would bid against each other—lowering their prices just to get work, and, in the process, lowering the floor for everyone.

One day, someone new came to the corner, a recruiter from the Latino Union. He had news of an alternative.

Workers could come into the Albany Park Workers Center, a project of the Latino Union. There, they'd be protected from Chicago's brutal winter weather and from the summer's scorching sun. They could help themselves to coffee. There was a bathroom—no ducking into the McDonald's, no facing curious and sometimes hostile glances from neighbors wondering about these "outsiders" crowded on the sidewalk.

Employers could call the center. There was a list of workers, organized by skill. A coordinator—a Latino Union employee—would make the connection, according to a protocol voted on by the worker members of the Latino Union. Then, the worker and employer would negotiate wages, working conditions, hours, and payment method. There wasn't a fee for the service—not for the employer, not for the worker. The worker would show up, contract in hand, and both employer and worker would sign. If all went well, there'd be repeat jobs and referrals.

"Most of the clients I have right now, I got through the worker center. They call me again and again and again," Nieto said.

For Nieto, the Albany Park Workers Center made a difference. In his fifties, Nieto, a skilled remodeler who left Mexico more than twenty years ago, no longer wanted to work the heavy labor jobs. But, at the corner, he'd have no choice. With seventy or eighty men desperate for work, there'd be no opportunity to be picky. Take what you get, or get moving. Nieto had a strategy of standing a little off to the side, knowing that as much as he didn't like dealing with the throng, some employers felt the same way. Even so, there were no guarantees.

On the corners, the men in trucks were often contractors, or more likely, subcontractors to subcontractors. Whatever their intentions were about paying, they'd only be able to pay if they got paid, and sometimes everyone was out of money. And those were the good guys. Others were just out-and-out crooks, never intending to pay for labor received.

It happened to Nieto more than once—three years ago, someone didn't pay him $9,000 for work on a basement. Since then, with the help of Latino Union, he's received $5,000 and may get more.

The people who called into the worker center were generally homeowners. They had a job, they'd negotiate the pay, and there was more of a chance of getting paid. "Here you get a contract, so if you don't get paid, you can fight for your wages," he said. "But on the corner, you had nothing."

On a summer day in August 2019, Nieto, who had just finished a bathroom makeover, stopped by the Latino Union to eat and say goodbye to the employer coordinator, Jose Flores Sanchez, who was leaving to study public policy in New York.

A mound of chopped cilantro scented the room of Latino Union's double storefront, just off a main street lined with

Mexican *supermercados* and *taquerillas* in Chicago's working-class Albany Park neighborhood.

"We spend so much on food," the Latino Union's director, Analía Rodríguez, had complained half-heartedly just moments before describing *comida* as an important organizing tool, along with political analysis, health and safety training, and child care. Outside, on a grill set up curbside, a member turned slices of seasoned beef and warmed tortillas next to a lineup of roasting corn.

The Latino Union's Albany Park hiring hall got its start when neighbors began complaining about the workers gathering at the local McDonald's. "There were a lot of issues with the police, with some neighbors, you know, harassing them and trying to kick them out," Rodríguez said.

She described the neighbors' complaints: "*They were upset. These men are standing here. They are blocking the sidewalk. There is danger. There is danger crossing the street.* There are always issues that the men come from outside, from the outside into *our* neighborhood. *They are coming to look for work and dirtying our streets.*

"In reality, these men are actually from the neighborhood," she said. "The men who stand waiting for work on specific corners, they are actually from the area. It's not like they are traveling miles to come to work."

The Latino Union attempted mediation. "We were trying to figure out with the city, with the streets, with the neighbors, but there was not really much we could move," she said. "The Latino Union sought private funding and opened up the Albany Park Workers Center."

It took four years of study and development. Then, in 2004, the Latino Union opened its hall for day laborers, primarily working in construction and landscaping. In March 2016, the Latino Union expanded the hiring hall to include housekeepers.

It wasn't as simple as opening the doors and putting on the coffee. The job process had to be transparent and equitable. "At the corner, everyone just rushes. You are negotiating against each other and bringing down wages," Rodríguez said. Instead, the goal was collaboration. The workers, for example, had to set minimum prices, so they wouldn't duplicate the underbidding so common on the corners.

"We had to develop guidelines," she said. "How were we going to keep each other accountable? What kind of rules do we need to have to have a safe space?"

The workers devised a system where they would list their skills—painting, carpentry, masonry. Employers could call in between 8 a.m. and noon and speak to a coordinator. Then the coordinator would make a connection based on skills.

"The coordinators aren't construction workers or domestic workers," Rodríguez explained. They don't know how to do the job, but they make the connection. Direct negotiations between employer and worker follow, by phone or email, covering time, scope of work, and materials.

"If both parties agree, then there's a written contract that the workers take with them," she said. "The employer knows that the worker is bringing a contract, and both will sign before the job starts. Then the worker goes about the job and gets paid directly. There is no fee for the employer. There is no fee for the worker. The whole point is to make sure each worker gets a new client and in return, that client starts referring them to other people."

Rodríguez said employers who like a particular worker can continue the relationship outside of the hiring hall. Or they can call in to request a specific worker.

About fifteen workers a month use the hiring hall, with more coming in the winter as summer construction and landscaping jobs shut down. In summer, workers tend to remain with one employer throughout the season.

The Latino Union is no temp agency disguised as a nonprofit, Rodríguez said. Its mission of worker empowerment at the intersection of immigration and labor remains paramount.

"The Latino Union is a membership organization," Rodríguez

explained. "In order to use the hiring hall, you can come and just try it out, but after that you have to actually become a member. A few years ago, we became more strict about that. What that meant is that they have to pay $30 in annual dues, and they have to commit to attending six events a year—so that can include training, meetings, and rallies. They have to commit to the mission and values of the Latino Union."

Those values have led to big wins for the worker center and its members. Founded in 2000 by women temporary workers, Latino Union pushed Chicago to pass a Day Labor Ordinance in 2002. With others, the worker center pushed the same concept statewide, resulting in the 2005 Day Laborer Protection Act, which regulates temporary agencies.

The Latino Union was behind a 2005 Illinois task force on Latino workplace injuries and fatalities; statistics show that Latino workers are at disproportionate risk. The Latino Union worked with the media to draw attention to May Day immigrants' rights marches in 2006 and 2007. In 2007, when Illinois raised its minimum wage, the worker center advocated to make sure its provisions would apply to 300,000 temporary workers originally not covered by the bill.

In 2008, again working at the intersection of immigration and labor, Latino Union helped facilitate a state law protecting immigrant residents from documentation-based discrimination. Public outreach and education led to statewide protection against wage theft in 2010. "In 2011, Latino Union completed a three-year NIOSH (U.S. National Institute for Occupational Safety and Health) workplace health and safety training program that trained 500 low-wage contingent workers," according to the worker center's website.

At about that same time, Latino Union began organizing caregivers, nannies, and housekeepers. Those efforts paid off on January 1, 2017, when the Illinois Domestic Workers' Bill of Rights Act took effect. Latino Union, working with other worker center groups, made it possible for domestic workers, long excluded from the state's fair labor standards act, to receive minimum wages, overtime, a day of rest a week, and the right to file harassment and discrimination claims.

The worker center organizes what it calls *Café y Charla* (Coffee and Chats) about the important issues. "We have different topics we bring to the workers, and that's where the education piece comes in," Rodríguez said. With some members active in those sweeping initiatives, others choose to deal with matters close at hand, including the nuts and bolts of running a hiring hall, making policy at monthly meetings.

What happens, for example, if a worker lies about his skill level and botches the assignment? When it happened, other workers made good on the job—after all, the center's reputation was at stake.

"This year, I told them how much money we have in the budget to market the hiring hall," Rodríguez said. It'll be up to the membership to figure out how to use it.

"Most of our membership are immigrants, so a lot of the abuses come because they are more vulnerable because of their status. Sometimes we hear things like 'I'm not going to pay you because you are undocumented. If you keep talking about wanting to have safety equipment on the job, we'll call ICE on you,'" Rodríguez said. "There's a lot of retaliation and a lot of abuse. Some employers actively seek immigrants because they'll be able to take advantage of them."

When employers call in asking for immigrants, the coordinator tells them the worker center doesn't ask about documentation, Rodríguez said. But if there's a problem, she's quick to get on the phone with the employer, mount a protest, or leaflet at the employer's home or business.

As much as Latino Union focuses on larger issues and the hiring hall, its members also count on it for community. Many work alone, tending babies or gardens.

"Here, they can support each other. For example, there are ESL classes once a week where they can come and learn English, very practical stuff, how to negotiate your salary, how to ask for a raise, things that people need to get by during work," Rodríguez said.

Latino Union member Arnoldo Corzandes, in his sixties, left Guatemala ten years ago to protect his sons from violence. He takes painting and gardening jobs through the worker center. But there's more to his membership than work. "We know each other and we enjoy the company and we try to improve ourselves," he said. "We are like family here."

Ahmed Ali, former executive director, Greater Minnesota
Worker Center, St. Cloud. *I. George Bilyk*

Lou Kimmel, executive director, New Labor,
New Brunswick, New Jersey. *Jane M. Von Bergen*

Part II

Challenges, Tensions

Worker centers represent a new horizon in the labor movement, but they are also organizations. And like all organizations, they have their challenges. How do they define their mission and set priorities? How do they build leadership? How do they manage resources? And, uniquely, how do worker centers relate to traditional mainstream labor unions? Are they allies, rivals, or somewhere in the middle?

> If you want to start a union, we can help you do it.
> —Pete Meyers, Tompkins County Workers' Center

> I wouldn't want to speculate about what is right or wrong with the union. I don't want to say anything about the union. I want to be respectful to them, but we do different work.
> —Alma Garcia, a pseudonym,
> Centro de Derechos Laborales

> We are still in pursuit of this new version of a union.
> —Carmen Martino, New Labor

6

IN THE SERVICE OF POWER

Milagros Barreto, organizer with the Immigrant Worker Center in Boston, likes to tell the story of Esther, a woman who sought help from the center five years ago. "She came in all black, no makeup. She had been crying for days," Barreto said, describing her first encounter with Esther. "She was walking with difficulty. She says, 'I need help. I got injured. I fell in my workplace and they fired me.'"

Esther had worked in an industrial bakery, moving bread from one part of the bakery to another. In the process, she fell and so badly hurt her knee that she could no longer work. "'They don't believe me. I'm in pain. I can hardly walk, and they just fired me because I don't have papers,'" Barreto said, quoting Esther.

"That shocked me," Barreto said. "We have to do something."

She lined Esther up with an attorney and encouraged her to come to meetings. Eventually, though, the worker center became more than doctors and lawyers for Esther. "She talked about it herself—how important it was to become a member of the worker center, so you don't feel alone," Barreto said. "You have support; there's support for all the members." For example, other members would invite Esther for coffee, easing her isolation.

Esther began to learn her rights. She encouraged other workers to join the Massachusetts Coalition for Occupational Safety and Health (MassCOSH), which runs the center as a program. Esther now stands at train stations and talks to potential members. "She became a different way," more confident, Barreto said. "She started accompanying workers to the doctors' appointments, and that was amazing. Then you start seeing her putting on lipstick and brushing her hair and we were like 'Wow, this is amazing.' I think she is the perfect example, but we have many, many examples."

Workers often come in with problems—immigration, wage theft, health and safety—but not all stay on as members, and fewer yet go on to lead as Esther did.

"We are focused on building the leadership of workers and empowering them. We are not caseworkers," said Jodi Sugerman-Brozan, executive director of MassCOSH. "We are organizing workers. We are not social service providers. We want workers to commit to being connected. We're dedicated to building a movement for worker justice, so we don't just want to provide them with an attorney and say goodbye. We want to build leadership, both within the campaigns and within our organization."

If there is any struggle that defines worker centers, it's the struggle of turning workers, troubled by their own individual stresses, into advocates and leaders, willing to help others gain power, strength, and justice on the job and in the community.

When workers knock on the door, it's not social change they are seeking. They just want to get paid, or maybe have a safer place to work.

For worker centers, it's a never-ending question of balance. Resources applied to helping individuals mean fewer resources for the larger struggle. Yet workers usually come to the centers for individual help. Centers perpetually endeavor to resolve the dilemma, but mostly they don't. Instead, what persists is a tension—sometimes an uneasy tension—between the worker center as a social service agency and the worker center as a builder of workplace and community power.

When Pete Meyers and Carl Feuer, a longtime activist in the Ithaca region, started the Tompkins County Workers' Center predecessor organization in 2003, they planned to harness community power to fulfill the mission of the organization's first name—Tompkins County Living Wage Coalition. They'd grab their wins wherever they could get them.

In 2006, Meyers and Feuer developed the first living wage certification program in the nation and changed the coalition's name to the Tompkins County Workers' Center.

But even in their earliest coalition days, Meyers and Feuer saw the importance of a worker hotline available for complaints about wages and other issues. In organizing circles, Meyers said, hotlines are controversial. "Some see the hotline as a service model, not as an organizing tool."

For the Tompkins County Workers' Center in upstate New York, it's been both. The specific issues raised by individual workers who call the center's hotline build participation, volunteerism, and leadership. The hotline also provides a snapshot of which issues concern workers most. A couple of well-publicized wage and hour cases that arose from calls to the hotline brought the center the recognition it needed in its early days.

By November 2018, though, the center was drowning, spending $20,000 of its $175,000 annual budget to assist workers in filing discrimination complaints with the state. Before that, the complaints had been handled by paralegals employed by the county's Office of Human Rights. Those positions are no longer funded.

"On one hand, it's good that there is a local organization that can do it," Meyers said. "But it has cost us money." Indeed, by November 2019, the center was down to its last $3,000, two staffers had been laid off, and Meyers's hours were cut from thirty-five to twenty. A last-minute fundraiser kept the doors open.

It's a dilemma.

Clearly, individual complaints bring workers in the door, but solving their issues takes resources, as Meyers can attest. That's one challenge. The second challenge is getting workers to stay active once their problems are resolved.

Many centers have attempted to deal with this conundrum

by requiring the workers to participate, at least while their cases are being handled. Arise Chicago and the Latino Union of Chicago charge membership dues, for example. Each year, Arise Chicago requires members to attend a certain number of events—organizational meetings, training workshops, and protests, all with the hope of increasing engagement and building leadership.

It doesn't always work.

Ania Jakubek, domestic worker organizer at Arise Chicago, had just finished a Saturday meeting with domestic workers at Arise's offices opposite Union Square. Relaxing after the August 2019 meeting, she pointed to one picture on the bulletin board—a smiling woman holding a big check, Jakubek at her side, smiling as well. The woman had been working twelve hours a day, five days a week on the overnight shift—no overtime—taking care of an elderly woman.

The elderly woman's sister argued that the worker didn't have any responsibilities while her client was asleep. The worker was owed $16,000. After Jakubek negotiated with the elderly woman's sister, the sister agreed to pay $11,000.

The worker asked Jakubek whether she should accept the $11,000, letting the $5,000 go. Jakubek told her, "I would take it, because, people giving you on the spot, $11,000, never happens." Also, legal fees would eat up a couple thousand dollars *if* the case were successful in court. The sister came in, had coffee with Jakubek, and wrote out a check.

"The next day, the [worker] came," Jakubek said. "I gave her the check. We took a picture. But you know what? She never came back."

Those experiences, though disheartening, don't deter Arise from its mission. Each month, domestic workers come to their regular Saturday meeting at the center. They've successfully worked with other groups, including the Latino Union, to push for a statewide domestic worker rights bill in Illinois. When it passed in 2016, guaranteeing domestic workers the minimum wage and other basic labor rights, "we were crying, all of us," with joy, said Chicago housekeeper Magdalena Zylinska, a leader in Arise Chicago's domestic worker group who testified before the Illinois state legislature.

Not every worker comes to a worker center with a job problem, but workers do come expecting needs to be met, as the founders of New Labor in New Brunswick, New Jersey, learned. It wasn't exactly what they expected. Twenty years ago, Carmen Martino and Rich Cunningham were hoping for a worker revolution. Instead they got a classroom.

Martino and Cunningham had sent recent college graduate Lou Kimmel to get hired by a temporary staffing agency so they could learn more about temp workers. They hoped that Kimmel, now New Labor's executive director, would bring them news about workers eager to build power on the job. Then Martino, Cunningham, and Kimmel would step in, organize the workers, and build solidarity, right out of a Labor 101 textbook.

Kimmel would report weekly to Cunningham, now deceased. "For about six months, we kept asking, 'What do they want? What do temp workers need?'" recalled Martino, now an assistant professor at Rutgers University. "And Lou would just say, 'Well, they want to learn how to speak English.' We asked, 'Okay, but what else?'" This went on for months as Kimmel unloaded trucks, tightened bottle caps, and de-weeded a pond, all as a temp worker.

"And there was never anything else. We wanted to organize through worker safety, but they wanted English lessons," Martino said.

So when New Labor opened its doors to workers, it began as a place to learn English.

New Labor found a classic "gateway" to membership, a strategy that is effective because it does not require direct confrontation with an employer.

"It's very scary for a worker to go after their current employer," said Carly Fox, a worker and immigrant advocate formerly with the Worker Justice Center of New York. "If we are at an organization to achieve worker rights, then we have to build community and build trust. We start with low hanging fruit."

That's why worker centers in central New York put so much energy into the successful statewide Green Light NY driver's license campaign. As of December 2019, drivers, regardless of immigration status, can now carry a driver's license, keeping them in compliance with the law. That way, immigrants can't be deported for driving without a license.

"These people can't drive to the store. A big issue is isolation. That's why the driver's license campaign resonates," Fox said, thinking particularly about workers scattered on farms. "All this isolation only leads to racism. Those human connections are what break through all this manufactured hate."

"It's a gateway issue," Fox said, one that unites workers across multiple industries, ethnic groups, and immigrant status, building connections and networks that can grow capacity later.

Lately, immigration issues have strained the balance between building worker power and service to individuals. Nothing trumps the threat of deportation, often causing workers to slide back into the shadows and accept abuse on the job.

At the Centro Laboral de Graton in California, instead of practicing talking to the boss about safety conditions, workers role-play what to do when U.S. Immigration and Customs Enforcement (ICE) knocks on the door.

At the Alianza Agricola, an alliance of agricultural workers in central and upstate New York, workers hold dances to raise money—not for worker campaigns, but to bail their members out of deportation centers. On August 30, 2018, Dairy Day at the New York State Fair, longtime dairy worker Carlos Cardona, cofounder and co-president of Alianza, was picked up while driving and handed over to the federal border patrol for not having a valid driver's license.

"We all knew it was only a matter of time before one of the members was going to get picked up," said Fox, who also worked with Alianza. "We had been throwing these dances to raise money for bail and thank God we did. We raised $10,000 for his bail. Those dances are why we had enough money to bail him out."

In Chicago, "we also organize at the intersection of labor and immigration," said Analía Rodríguez, executive director of the Latino Union of Chicago. "So then, if there are any issues with wage theft or immigration, if you are a member, of course, we're going to go in full capacity." Latino Union maintains connections with lawyers who can help members with immigration issues and separate connections with labor lawyers.

By contrast, Arise Chicago draws careful boundaries around the immigration issue.

"Even though there are all kinds of crises related to immigration, obviously, we're not doing things like citizenship workshops or detention relief, because that's outside of our mission," and there are other Chicago groups handling that work, said Adam Kader, director of Arise Chicago Worker Center. "We're pro–immigrant rights. But, in so far as our site of intervention—it's the workplace. If workers come to us with some kind of [immigration] issue, we refer it out to the groups that do it."

Arise Chicago stepped up during the summer of 2019 when the U.S. Social Security Administration sent letters to 570,000 businesses advising them to check a directory because names and social security numbers of some employees did not match the agency's records. Employers were firing some employees because of it, even though typographical errors sometimes can cause discrepancies. Arise mounted a campaign to alert workers. The campaign also reminded employers that they didn't have to respond to the "No Match" letters and that Social Security had directed that workers not be dismissed simply because of the letters.

"Other immigrant rights groups weren't doing anything on the No Match, nor should they," Kader said. "It's not really their expertise or their territory. We're the group that stepped up and said, 'This is the problem. This is the solution.'"

Meanwhile, the struggle to balance resources strains worker center budgets. Many operate on a shoestring, with annual budgets in the $100,000 to $200,000 range—enough to support a staff person or two, buy the coffee, and pay modest rent.[1]

For worker centers, funding is a constant juggling act—a grant here, a grant there. Some money may come from the U.S. Department of Labor, which, through its Occupational Safety and Health Administration, parcels out Susan Harwood Training Grants designed to teach low-literacy, underserved, and high-risk workers about health and safety, as well as rights and responsibilities on the job.

Grants come from unions. For example, the Service Employees International Union contributed to efforts to organize dairy workers and other kinds of employees in upstate New York through the Workers' Center of Central New York. Advocacy groups, such as Oxfam America, may step up. Oxfam has been funding campaigns to support centers dealing with working conditions in poultry plants.

Interfaith groups, such as the Catholic Campaign for Human Development, underwrite worker centers, as do foundations. Sometimes larger organizations, such as the Interfaith Worker Justice (IWJ) organization, will receive a large grant and, in turn, distribute it to worker centers to use locally. But those funding sources are tenuous. For example, in 2019, IWJ was in the process of reorganizing and transitioning away from direct financial support for worker centers.

Worker centers may help each other through collaborations, such as Green Light NY and coalitions in Boston and upstate New York. Some worker centers around the country belong to the

National Domestic Workers Alliance. In Chicago, eight worker centers chipped in to create Raise the Floor, which provides joint legal and public policy services.

"Raise the Floor is a great opportunity because it's greater than the sum of its parts," said Kader at Arise Chicago. "We're not just eight worker centers. We're also a ninth entity called Raise the Floor. It can give us more capacity and it can also help us orient our efforts and make a bigger splash."

"It's shared back-of-the-house resources," Kader said. "We don't have a joint insurance pool, but we have a legal department that we all share. We also have a public policy director at Raise the Floor that we can all borrow. It's a way to aggregate our efforts to a higher scale of activity. We don't have to be alone doing this. We're not replicating each other's work."

For example, Raise the Floor can organize a bus trip to the state capital, rent the bus, determine which advocates will visit which legislators, and deal with details as small as ordering food. "We show up. We do our job. We come back. We get the report. It's a huge capacity builder," Kader said.

"We're not going at cross-purposes with each other's work," he said. "We may be giving hell to one politician while another worker center is trying to work with them on a different issue. For all I know, a politician could be playing the two of us off [against] each other. If they are shrewd, that's what they'll be doing. Raise the Floor can manage those conflicts."

At the Latino Union, Analía Rodríguez agrees. At Raise the Floor meetings, she learns about worker issues in logistics and warehouses—issues her day laborer members in construction and her domestic workers in housekeeping don't bring up. She can tap into the legal department, and Raise the Floor's public policy director keeps her informed on the progress of legislation or on various campaigns, so she doesn't need to do that research herself.

"When I think of coalition work, I think of it like you are dating," said Rodríguez. When there are problems at the dating level, it's easy enough to say, " 'Okay, this is not working out. We're done. We're going to go our own ways.'

"But with Raise the Floor, we actually got married. We're committed for the good and the bad," Rodríguez said. "There are some struggles. We're all similar, but we're so different. The differences sometimes come into play when we have to organize a campaign. But that's also the beautiful part."

Worker center leaders find strength in collaboration. It's a strength they badly need. The stakes are high and the demands are never-ending. Relations with boards can be fraught with tension caused by differing visions and goals. For example, Houston's Fe y Justicia had four executive directors in eight years. Leadership disagreements in Bryan, Texas, led to changes at the top at the Centro de Derechos Laborales, the group helping poultry workers.

"Turnover is absolutely very high," said Martha Ojeda, senior national organizer with Interfaith Worker Justice.

"Many organizers are dealing with all the programs, and at the same time they have to do the fundraising, and do all the administration tasks, finances, payroll, and so on. Therefore, it is very intense," Ojeda said.

Pressures outside the realm of workplace struggles exacerbate the problem. A worker center may have embarked on a campaign to eradicate wage theft, but police harassment, deportation, travel restrictions, and other challenges intrude. Victories that once seemed close begin to slip away. Leaders got into the work to change the world, but the change they see seems small—and sometimes appears insignificant, given the effort. Yet the leader, although discouraged, can never show discouragement or fatigue.

Guilt is ever-present among leaders. How can they take a day off to throw birthday parties for their own children when wages are being stolen, when workers are being deported, when housekeepers are being sexually harassed, and when day laborers don't even have hardhats?

"You just stop putting boundaries," said Rebecca Fuentes, formerly the lead organizer and de facto executive director at the Workers' Center of Central New York (WCCNY) who left her position in December 2019. "Everything is for the cause. Everything is for the movement."

It's seductive—the work seems more meaningful and urgent than the day-to-day humdrum realities of laundry, dentist appointments, and birthday parties. Fuentes said she had neglected her marriage, her family, and her health in her ten years fighting to help New York's low-wage workers, particularly immigrant dairy hands. Even saying that, she said she felt guilty, knowing that WCCNY's immigrant worker members also miss their families and often suffer harsh conditions on the farms.

"I always felt guilty, even getting paid I felt guilty," she said. Now she helps workers as a volunteer, and only as a volunteer. "I'm going to a therapist. I'm losing weight," she said. "I'm trying to reclaim my life and my health and be a better partner to my husband."

Fuentes also faced internal issues within her organization and with several close allies, exacerbating her growing feeling of being burnt out. Because several key worker victories had been won, it felt like the right time to go.

"It's not the kind of work you can do in just eight hours. You work on the weekends, at night, because that is when workers are available," Ojeda said. "You can't just be sitting in the office waiting like everything will happen by magic. You need to be there when workers can talk. You put aside dinnertime with the family or spending time with your family on the weekends because you are doing this kind of work."

An important part of the job is cultivating worker leaders, but turnover is high among their ranks as well.

"The bank of workers you had a year ago is gone, it's constantly changing. All these workers are immigrants. They are not making a living wage and they don't have support. It's people who are just surviving day to day. They find a better job or their needs get bigger—they need to take care of their family, whatever," she said. "You can have a neighborhood that is really well organized and suddenly, people are deported, people move, and you have to start over with that place. It's the nature of the work."

Ojeda remembered a conversation she once had with an organizer she worked with in Mexico.

"I remember he was saying, 'Martha, I am so tired. I am preparing some leaders and then they go away. Then I need to prepare more leaders and they leave. I'm so tired and I don't know what to do.'

"And I said, 'You know, maybe right now your short-term goal is building some leaders and those leaders are going away. But in the long-term, whatever happens, wherever they go, they are going to do the right thing.

" 'They are going to take the side of the workers,' " Ojeda told the discouraged organizer, perhaps as she struggled to overcome her own fatigue. Those leaders lost to the group now are going to defend workers' rights in the future, wherever they are, and they will have the skills to do it.

" 'You are raising consciousness for all of these people,' " she reminded the organizer. 'You are changing lives.'

" 'All these workers, all this knowledge, they are getting to be agents for social change,' " Ojeda said. " 'Wherever they go, lives change, and they are going to know the right thing to do.' "

7

UNEASY TENSION

For months, the tension had been building in Bryan, Texas, where the Centro de Derechos Laborales (CDL) represents poultry workers at Sanderson Farms, one of the biggest employers in Brazos County. So does the United Food and Commercial Workers Union Local 455. The plant's union representatives negotiated all the usual wages and benefits, including them in collective bargaining agreements. But where were those union reps, CDL's leaders wondered, when workers were injured on the job?

And where were they on October 1, 2018, when CDL staged a protest outside the plant complete with made-for-television visuals?

No one saw a union official joining protesters outside the plant wearing diapers, the way CDL's members and allies did to underscore the desperate situation workers experienced inside, where they were unable to get off the line to go to the bathroom. No union officials gave a speech or held a poster as workers complained about harsh chemicals used to disinfect chicken carcasses or the relentless production line speeds that lead to painful back, wrist, and shoulder injuries.

Where were they? The answer is complicated and speaks to a larger underlying tension in the labor movement.

Are established labor unions allies of worker centers? Are they rivals? Do they swoop in and take over after the worker centers do the hard work of organizing the marginalized? Or are they mentors and supporters, providing dollars and know-how, sometimes openly, sometimes behind the scenes? If labor unions and worker centers align on issues such as combating wage theft, they can also divide dramatically. That's what happened behind the scenes at the Bryan protest in what is almost a textbook example of existing tensions.

"I wouldn't want to speculate about what is right or wrong with the union," said Alma Garcia, then one of CDL's two part-time staffers. (Garcia is a pseudonym used at her request to protect her from retaliation.) "I don't want to say anything about the union. I want to be respectful to them, but we do different work."

From CDL's perspective, the workers' complaints about bathroom breaks and line speed had fallen on deaf ears. So CDL decided to hold its own rally, bringing in allies from worker centers in Arkansas and North Carolina, both home to major poultry companies. Also donning diapers were representatives from the Southern Poverty Law Center, Oxfam America, Interfaith Worker Justice, Nebraska Appleseed, and the National Council for Occupational Safety and Health (National COSH). They were part of a coalition founded several years earlier to improve working conditions in U.S. poultry plants.

Besides, for five years, CDL had been hearing about safety problems at the plant. The problems were real. They'd *talked* a lot about them, but it was time for some *action*. CDL staff knew the demonstration was going to be an important tactic for the young organization. It was going to be their first public show of power and solidarity. Canceling would have been devastating.

UFCW Local 455 did not participate or endorse the October 1, 2018, demonstration, but they didn't try to stop it. It was a gesture by Local 455 that acknowledged the relationship that CDL has with workers, particularly the Spanish-speaking immigrant workforce. CDL had created a trusted space for poultry workers to discuss working conditions and develop skills to do something to improve them.

But Local 455 officials weren't happy, and neither were their national leaders in Washington. They felt blindsided. UFCW was part of that poultry worker coalition, but UFCW's officials in Washington didn't know about the rally. They questioned the coalition's decision. The UFCW staff knew relations between the Local 455 leadership and some workers were chilly, but worried that a protest about working conditions could destroy the union's credibility—with its members and with the company. Local 455 was in the middle of negotiations with Sanderson Farms, trying to resolve contentious issues, including a policy prohibiting union reps from accessing the plant. Why undermine the union, when unions—not worker centers—can compel employers to negotiate through the National Labor Relations Act?

By contrast, in upstate New York, Pete Meyers, who heads the Tompkins County Workers' Center, actually created a union local and walked the workers through their first contract. As he organized workers in the Ithaca Health Alliance, he arranged for them to join a union—Workers United, SEIU Regional Joint Board, in Rochester, New York. The union chartered a new local for them, Local 2833. That same local later included baristas from a nearby coffee chain, also organized by Meyers and the worker center.

Also, unlike the CDL members in Bryan, dairy workers in upstate New York were so adamant that a union would help them that they lobbied hard—and successfully—to persuade New York's legislature to overturn a state law prohibiting them from unionizing. Governor Andrew Cuomo signed the bill into law in July 2019.

By 2018, Rebecca Fuentes, then lead organizer with the Workers' Center of Central New York (WCCNY) in Syracuse, had come to believe that a union and a negotiated contract are key to lasting change. "We used to say dignity and respect," Fuentes said. Now, she believes, "dignity, respect, and a union." With a union, she said, "you have dignity, you have respect, and you have the power."

These days, the WCCNY is receiving support from a large union and has a union official on its board. But the worker center doesn't want to publicize the name of the union. It's a union that stands behind many worker campaigns across the nation, but often likes to keep in the background.

In Chicago, when several employees working for the same company come to Arise Chicago Worker Center for help, Arise tries its best to shepherd them into a union, with the union helping to move the group through the election and first-contract process. But Arise chooses its union partners carefully, explained Adam Kader, the center's director.

Union partners must sign an affirmation of Arise's labor values. "We want to affirm our values as an interfaith workers' rights organization. This is our vision for the labor movement. We think workers' participation should be maximized. We think we should be bold in our demands," Kader said.

"We don't want to just hand them off as a referral. We want to work together with the union to make sure it's a successful campaign," he said.

Many unions represent particular types of workers, such as masons, pilots, or teachers. But worker centers evolve to meet the needs of the workers at hand in an immediate community, such as Mexican dairy workers, immigrant prep cooks, Somali poultry workers, or Polish housekeepers. Many centers settle into niches over time as they become more focused on sets of workers by ethnic group or become more expert on specific wage or health and safety issues arising from worker complaints.

Mainstream unions employ researchers, policy analysts, political directors, health benefit administrators—and organizers. They hire lawyers to advise them on the massive amounts of regulatory paperwork required by the federal government.

Worker centers, on the other hand, don't carry as much

regulatory burden or overhead. They don't negotiate contracts or file multiple required reports with the U.S. Department of Labor.

Some anti-union groups and business trade associations say that worker centers are unions in every way except in name. The U.S. Chamber of Commerce calls worker centers "union front groups,"[1] and the Center for Union Facts claims worker centers are "organized labor's latest scheme to unionize workers without having to comply with federal labor laws."[2]

The U.S. Labor Department doesn't agree, ruling several times that worker centers don't fall under federal regulations requiring unions to report their finances. Still some business groups and their friends in Congress continue, so far unsuccessfully, to press the point. It's a concern for worker centers.

"Far from being high-paid union operatives, the people working at these worker centers are just people dedicated to getting a fair deal, fair wages, and safe working conditions for workers, and I don't think they have anything to fear from having more light shed on them," said Tom O'Connor, former executive director of the National Council for Occupational Safety and Health. "In fact, I think it might help them."

Without the regulatory burden unions carry, worker centers can spend their hours and energy creating innovative programs like the living wage certification devised by the Tompkins County Workers' Center. Even as worker centers struggle to keep the lights on and the doors open, they still manage to help smaller groups of workers who don't have the wherewithal to support the sophisticated infrastructures required by unions.

But worker center victories can be short-lived: a hard-fought agreement won in the worker centers' court of public opinion can fade away when cameras leave or key players among employers and employees move on. Worker centers often rely heavily on the energy of their founders and may not have the organizational resilience to survive once the founders leave. Even the widely heralded passage of laws pursued by worker centers that benefit tens of thousands of workers doesn't mean there is muscle available to enforce them. A collective bargaining contract, at least, assures some protections for the relatively few numbers of workers covered.

"I think that worker centers and unions are in conversation. We're being informed by each other's work," said Arise's Kader. "Arise's vision for its work with labor unions is that it's complementary. We're not here to replace labor unions. We're here to complement them and vice versa, because there's a whole diversity of workplaces covered by a whole breadth of law. There's not just a one-size-fits-all solution."

For example, Kader used to work at Latino Union of Chicago, eight miles north. That group primarily represents day laborers and domestic workers—mostly individuals working for individuals or small businesses. These aren't the type of workers typically covered by a collective bargaining agreement.

Latino Union's executive director, Analía Rodríguez, said her organization has a good relationship with the Chicago Labor Federation, affiliated with the AFL-CIO, the nation's largest labor federation. "At this point, there is nothing we are doing together. But we're there and the door is open," she said.

Still, she said, there is tension as the building trades worry about the day laborers bringing down wages. "The end goal will be how can we, as the Latino Union, have these conversations with unions to make sure we're all organizing for fair wages," Rodríguez said. "What does that cooperation look like? These hiring halls, these corners where the people are standing—this is their place of work. I think it's a matter of how we can collaborate and make sure we raise the floor for everyone."

Raising the floor for everyone is on Arise's mind as it leads members into unions. "We want a partner that we feel good about, that we are confident that they can represent the workers and that we have a good working relationship—so where we can have a degree of influence, frankly," Kader said. "It's having the union open to listening to us because our strength is the community organizing playbook. We know how to analyze an employer target and figure out where the pressure points are and push them."

But isn't that what unions do as well?

Not always, he replied. "Unions have been on the decline for a long time. They've been weakened significantly. Their budgets are cut. They're accustomed to a defensive stance, not an offensive stance. I think that worker centers bring a fighting and analytical perspective."

Labor unions are now looking to worker center tactics for their renewal and their organizing strategies, Kader said.

"We understand the labor movement as encompassing organized unionized workers and unorganized non-union workers," he said. "You'll hear some young worker center types saying things like 'Unions are old hat and we're the new wave.' We strongly disagree with that.

"We believe that worker centers are a recent evolution of the labor movement, but the future of the labor movement includes both."

8

A LATTE AND A UNION

Order a latte at Gimme! Coffee in a brick building on Cayuga Street, and the barista steaming the milk will be different from baristas in other coffee shops in the college town of Ithaca, New York, and indeed, different from baristas across the nation. That's because the baristas at Gimme! Coffee are union members, covered under a collective bargaining agreement negotiated between the owner and their union, Workers United Local 2833. The baristas, who pour coffee at several cafés in the Ithaca area, believe they were the first baristas in the nation to be unionized.

"For me, the most integral part of this has been to see how far my co-workers and I have come in building solidarity, in rebalancing power and having the courage to take action and create a better workplace," barista Samantha Mason said in a statement after the group ratified its first contract, in February 2018. "It's important to me that all workers understand that they can change their workplace." [1]

Workers understanding that they can change their workplaces? That's what a labor movement is, and for the baristas in Ithaca, it started at the Tompkins County Workers' Center, when two baristas walked in the door and wanted to talk to someone about problems they had been experiencing at work.

The Tompkins County Workers' Center isn't a union. It doesn't have the structure, the financial support, the government regulations, or the deep leadership bench. It doesn't have much staff or a big budget—just about $175,000 yearly. But for fifteen years, the very fact that the center wasn't a labor union helped give it the nimbleness to address workers' needs and allowed it to innovate in ways that wouldn't fit into a typical union structure.

The Tompkins County Workers' Center, for example, not only organized baristas into a union, but, in 2006, developed the nation's first living wage certification program, a model being duplicated in other states. The center has awarded 118 companies a certificate in recognition of their willingness to pay at least $15.11 an hour, the amount needed to sustain a modest lifestyle in Ithaca and its surroundings.

"It's a challenge to be that nimble," noted Pete Meyers, the center's coordinator.

Unions amass thick bureaucracies and are governed by the National Labor Relations Act (NLRA). Worker centers, on the other hand, don't carry as much regulatory overhead.

The two Gimme! Coffee baristas met Meyers at the center's office in a comfortably run-down co-working loft shared by a half-dozen nonprofits in a building that also houses a vegan café and a used bookstore.

"It's rare when we get two workers from the same place. They already had protected concerted activity," Meyers said, legal-speak for the NLRA's interpretation of the constitutionally guaranteed freedom of association. That freedom allows workers to meet together, union or not, "for the purpose of . . . mutual aid or protection."

To help the baristas and their co-workers, Meyers relied on relationships built up over the years in Ithaca, including his connection with the coffee shops' owner, Kevin Cuddeback.

Cuddeback, Meyers said, had started down the traditional union-avoidance path, forcing his workers into meetings—not really in keeping with the image he projected to the public. "The owner puts himself out as a Bernie Sanders type," Meyers said, referring to the U.S. senator from Vermont who was running for president in 2020 on a left-leaning platform. "We asked him to remain neutral." Cuddeback did, and won kudos from Meyers and the baristas.

Meyers also introduced the baristas to leaders of Workers United Local 2833. He knew the local's leaders well, because Local 2833 didn't exist until Meyers connected unhappy administrative workers from the Ithaca Health Alliance to a union, Workers United, SEIU Regional Joint Board, in Rochester, New York.

When the workers organized in 2014, they became the Rochester Regional Joint Board's newest local, Local 2833.

"When all the workers signed up to create their Local, it was Pete Meyers who went to the employer asking for recognition of the [Rochester Regional Joint Board] on the behalf of the workers—and the employer, the Ithaca Health Alliance, agreed," Workers United organizing consultant Richard Bensinger said in the union's newsletter.[2]

The center's expertise, Meyers said, lies in always looking to respond in a way that leads all kinds of workers—whether they be baristas or healthcare staffers—to more collective power. "Imagine that in a ten-day period, seven different baristas came in and we treated them all as individuals, as opposed to saying, it sounds like it makes sense to organize."

"If you want to start a union," he said, "we can help you do it." Meyers sees worker centers as allies, even incubators, of traditional unions.

Pete Meyers didn't come to upstate New York to turn baristas into union members. He arrived in Ithaca in 2000, to help single mothers navigate the welfare-to-work pathway on behalf of Catholic Charities. Meyers, who grew up in South Bend, Indiana, managed to get the mothers on his caseload into jobs, but, as it turned out, his success wasn't as successful for the mothers and their children.

"They were getting kicked into minimum-wage jobs," but weren't earning enough to sustain themselves or their families, Meyers said. His work felt futile. Why bother? At about that time, he met Carl Feuer, a longtime activist in the region who, in 1997, had founded the Living Wage Coalition. Together, in January 2003, the two men co-created the Tompkins County Workers' Center with the idea of advocating for a statewide living wage.

Living wage advocacy has given the center credibility and a voice throughout upstate New York. Individual workplaces can be wretched, but each is wretched in its own way. Yet every worker who gets a paycheck wants to earn enough to pay rent, buy food, connect to the internet, and have a little extra for fun and for savings. It makes a difference in the larger economy as well.

"Having a holistic issue that is appealing to workers and the public is important," Meyers said.

A few months after Meyers and Feuer started the center, they began the hotline. A couple of well-publicized wage and hour cases that came in through the hotline brought the center the recognition it needed in its early days.

Someone called in and tipped the center that Mexican immigrants at College Town Pizza were living in a basement and being paid well below the minimum wage, earning $300 a week when they should have been paid more than $470. Then a crusading New York State attorney general, Eliot Spitzer issued a strongly worded press release and ordered the pizzeria's owners to pay $7,230 in restitution. Not a huge amount. Not a big case. But in a college town like Ithaca, pizza parlor perfidy makes news.

A few years later, it was a college town coffee shop that made headlines, when a cashier reached out to the center after learning that the café's "backroom" workers—the Latino dishwashers, busboys, and others—weren't being paid or given days off. The center helped the young woman file a case with the New York State Department of Labor in 2009.

"It turned out that there were twenty people living in an apartment and they hadn't been paid for six months," Meyers said.

In September 2010, the department fined the owner $623,000 for violations in his Ithaca café and another $377,000 for the

deli he owned in New York City. But by then it was too late. Six
months earlier, he had filed for bankruptcy and shut his doors.
The workers never got their back wages.[3] Now the center is helping to advocate for proposed state legislation that would expand
wage protections for workers through liens and insurance.

"To be clear, while living wage was the beginning of our organization, in the last ten years, there have been a whole wealth of
issues, not only what [workers] are taking home, but what they
are experiencing on the job," Meyers said. Still, the center hasn't
strayed far from its original mission. Its innovative living wage
certification program not only protects workers, but moves their
bosses closer to a vision of economic equity.

"Our national social and economic life suffers from cold cur-
rents of despair, poverty, drug addiction and other ills connected
to low wages," the center wrote on its website when it announced
a certification for Crispin Brotherton Construction, LLC. The
website noted that Brotherton, the owner, grew up in poverty.
"Crispin Brotherton likes to think of a local living wage as plant-
ing a sturdy hedge around our community, that offers some protection from the howling winds of corporate greed."

On its application, the company wrote, "We like the idea of
thriving together."

Meyers said the center doesn't examine companies' books, but
will withdraw certification if it receives complaints. So far, two
companies have lost certification.

Meyers, who is also a leader of the Upstate New York Workers'
Centers Alliance, finds himself intrigued by the analogy of decen-
tralized leadership and focus as outlined in *The Starfish and the
Spider: The Unstoppable Power of Leaderless Organizations*, by Ori
Brafman.

The Tompkins County Workers' Center isn't a leaderless organization, but the way it organizes itself around issues reminds
Meyers more of the starfish than the spider.

"If you cut a spider in half, it dies," Meyers explained, the way the center would if it relied on just one issue or just one person. But that's not how it has been, or will be, as far as Meyers is concerned.

"If you cut off a starfish's arm," Meyers said, "it lives and it keeps growing."

9

"THEY WANTED A REVOLUTION"

Angel Fernandez could have been Magdalena Pulla's son—the age is about right. But Pulla's own son, Andres Aguilar, was with her on Sunday, marching through the tired streets of New Brunswick, New Jersey. Together they were chanting, "Not one death more" during the annual march for El Día de los Trabajadores Caídos—Worker Memorial Day—on April 28, 2019, sponsored in part by New Labor, a worker center in town.

Angel Fernandez wasn't with them. The twenty-seven-year-old construction worker had died about six weeks earlier. On March 12, Fernandez, who had been living in Union City, New Jersey, fell from a roof at a construction site in nearby Union Township. He left behind two children, ages seven and ten.

It's not that every immigrant from every country knows every other immigrant from the same country, even when they settle close by in a small state like New Jersey. But there are networks, so Pulla, through relatives, knew Fernandez's family. Both came from Ecuador; they had the immigrant's dream in common—the drive to come to the United States to build a better life for their families. Pulla understands that well.

Maybe that's why her voice caught as she addressed a group of about 250 gathered for the service for the fallen workers at Anshe Emeth Memorial Temple in New Brunswick.

"Today is a very sad day," she said, speaking about Fernandez through a translator. "We have memories of our husbands, fathers, children, and friends who are injured at their workplaces and sometimes even died.

"Three years ago, he came to the United States with many dreams, with ideals, so he could provide for his children," she said. Fernandez lost his dreams, she said, along with his life. His "children have lost their dream as well, that their dad would build them a house and help them with their studies."

For New Labor, El Día de los Trabajadores Caídos Reunión y Marcha, the Worker Memorial Day march, is an important event. It's a day to rally its members, people like Magdalena Pulla, who mobilize workers for New Labor.

Most of New Labor's members are Latino low-wage workers, so El Día reminds them, and others, of the importance of their work and what's at stake. It's not just wages and working conditions, although those certainly matter. It's as fundamental as human life—the life of a father, a father like Angel Fernandez.

Since New Labor began nearly twenty years ago, more than four thousand people like Pulla have paid dues to the worker center, with about five hundred paying yearly. New Labor can boast three offices around the state—in New Brunswick, Newark, and Lakewood—and an impressive list of public policy initiatives, either advocated on its own or as leaders in partnerships with others.

In Lakewood, New Labor's efforts are focused on domestic workers. In 2013, New Labor managed to push the town council to pass a resolution, the "Bill of Rights for Domestic Workers." "Domestic workers are hard to organize," said New Labor's unassuming executive director, Lou Kimmel. "Workers clean multiple houses in a day. They don't have one employer, so they came up with their own bill of rights.

"The biggest issue is around knees," he said. "They don't want to work on their knees because it's humiliating. They don't want someone watching over them and telling them to go down on their knees and clean. It's more about respect."

In Newark, the focus is construction, and in New Brunswick, New Labor's headquarters, temp, warehouse, and restaurant workers form the largest groups of members. In 2015, New Labor made headlines when it helped temp workers recover $100,000 in back wages from a staffing agency doing business as Olympus Management Services, Atlantis Personnel, and other names. New Jersey froze the companies' assets when the companies' workers' compensation insurance carrier reported to state officials that the staffing agency had been misrepresenting the number of workers they employed to avoid paying higher premiums. In the process, paychecks for as many as eight hundred workers were also frozen.

New Labor organized marches and protests, while working behind the scenes with government officials to unlock the money and amend an arbitrary cut-off date. Then, New Labor mobilized to find the workers, so they could recoup their wages. It took about eight months for workers to get paid. "But rent doesn't wait," Kimmel said. New Labor found about 150 of the unpaid workers in two separate outreach efforts.

Throughout the state, New Labor has been the chief advocate behind four municipal wage theft bills and a strong ally in two others. New Labor particularly pushed wage theft bills in Princeton, Newark, Highland Park, and New Brunswick.

Wage theft occurs in many ways. Sometimes checks bounce or an employer simply disappears without issuing paychecks. Sometimes people work all day and aren't paid at the end, and there's no immediate recourse. The next day, the boss is nowhere to be found. Sometimes workers are shorted—paid for fewer hours or days than they worked or paid at less than the minimum wage or are cheated out of overtime pay. The variations on the theme are many, but the bottom line remains the same—workers not being paid for their labor.

In New Brunswick's law—passed on December 18, 2013— enforcement is tied to an annual renewal of an operating license. If there's a court finding that wages are owed, employers must pay up or they won't be able to renew their licenses. Next, New Labor advocated for a statewide wage theft measure. It was signed into law in June 2019.

The worker center also pushed for the statewide Earned Paid Sick Leave Law. Passed in 2018, the act allows employees to accrue up to forty hours of paid sick leave per year to be used to care for themselves or family members. Significantly, the law covers temp workers, a key New Labor constituency. Even if temp workers go on assignment to different companies, they accrue sick leave through the agency that places them.

On February 4, 2019, New Jersey governor Phil Murphy signed into law an act designed to get most New Jersey workers to a minimum wage of $15 an hour by 2024. One of the groups lobbying for it? New Labor.

Still on New Labor's to-do list is a bill to improve working conditions for temp workers. The idea is to augment worker center efforts in Massachusetts, which, in 2013, led to the Temporary Workers Right to Know Act and, in Illinois, the Responsible Job Creation Act, which went into effect on June 1, 2018.

Those laws require staffing agencies to provide temporary workers with basic information—hourly wage, nature of the work, type of equipment and chemicals being used, and the actual name and owners of the temporary staffing agencies hiring them. Different laws have different additional provisions—no fees for background checks, guaranteed transportation, priority for permanent employment.

Kimmel said New Labor wants to add wage bonding and wage parity, with the bonds making sure workers get paid if the staffing agency closes. Also temp workers doing the same job as full-time employees should get the same rate, Kimmel said, sitting outside the New Jersey Department of Labor & Workforce Development's building in Trenton, the state capital, where he and other allies had gathered to talk to government officials about temporary worker issues.

"Temp work is devalued," he said. "It should be flipped. It should be value-added."

In other words, if a company needs temp workers to resolve a pressing staffing situation, it should cost the employer more than simply hiring enough workers to do the job.

All the advocacy adds up to a busy calendar for New Labor, which can trace its roots back nearly twenty years to the meeting of a longtime labor leader—cynical and sarcastic—who had gotten disillusioned with unions, and a young idealistic left-leaning college student.

That young idealistic left-leaning college student? Kimmel, now older, with hair beginning to turn gray. The longtime labor leader? Carmen Martino, now an assistant professor at Rutgers University and co-director of the Rutgers Occupational Training and Education Consortium.

Martino, who remembers picking berries on his grandparents' blueberry farm in southern New Jersey, became an air-conditioning refrigeration mechanic after he dropped out of college. "My mom said I had to learn something." After graduating from trade school, he landed work as a mechanic at an Atlantic City casino joining the union. When the union went on strike, Martino quit and went back to college.

"We had a dismal loss," he said about the strike. "I didn't want to be bothered with the union, actually. The union didn't do its job. It made a leftist out of me. But I did learn union principles from a guy who was a shop steward there."

Martino eventually earned a master's degree in labor studies from Rutgers in New Brunswick. "I began to think that maybe we could fix the union movement, so to speak."

The question was how. And then, in 1991, in one of those chance circumstances that changes everything, Martino saw the path.

Michael Merrill, one of Martino's professors, asked Martino to videotape five days of train-the-trainer safety and health training for the Oil, Chemical and Atomic Workers (OCAW) union. "What I saw in that five days convinced me that I should be doing this kind of work," Martino said. Martino was particularly struck by the training methodology utilized by the OCAW. Known as the Small Group Activity Method, it relies on workers teaching themselves and each other how to conduct their own safety analyses and develop their own problem-solving capacity.

"It can save somebody's life potentially," Martino said, talking about the safety training. "Increasingly, that's the case for low-wage workers. I mean, I know a lot of people who go to bed at night, thinking that's why we do this. And there's nothing wrong with that.

"But when I saw the Small Group Activity Method, I saw the potential here to take education and empowerment and put them together in the same room," he said. "What it does is lay the foundation for people to think and problem-solve collectively at work. That's what a union is—people working together to solve their own problems."

Through that training he met Tony Mazzocchi, a longtime OCAW health and safety advocate, who like Martino, wanted to strengthen labor. Mazzocchi's plan: build support for a new political party, the Labor Party. Martino signed on to help.

The Labor Party had its founding convention in 1996, and by 1998, Martino had taken leadership positions in the OCAW and the New Jersey Industrial Union Council. Momentum for the Labor Party faded after Mazzocchi's death, but the training method he championed never lost its allure for Martino.

During that time, the New Jersey Industrial Union Council, in partnership with Rutgers University's Occupational Safety and Health Project (OSHEP) had a long-standing health and safety worker training grant, which Martino and a union colleague, Rich Cunningham, shepherded out of offices in New Brunswick. On his commute, Martino "started to notice, driving in the very, very early mornings, lines of people that were waiting at temp agencies that had just basically sprung up overnight," he said. "All these people were getting jobs at warehouses that were literally being built and were just opening, right off Exit 8A."

He and Cunningham became curious—though their curiosity remained unsatisfied for a time.

Besides curiosity, they shared two other important attributes— enthusiasm for the Small Group Activity Method and a pressing urgency to redefine what was possible for the flagging labor movement. "I would just say about why we ended up with New Labor is because I was disillusioned. The unions in New Jersey were all falling apart," Martino said. "The industrial unions were disappearing rapidly, and it just seemed it was no longer a vehicle for workers—at least not in its current state. It was going away."

He and Cunningham reached the conclusion that "there needed to be a new kind of union and a new vehicle to adapt to the changes that were happening very rapidly in the workplace." Martino and Cunningham were promoting an economic analysis class they and others developed titled "Corporate Power and the American Dream." A lecture was delivered at Drew University in Madison, New Jersey. In the audience was a young and impressionable student, Lou Kimmel, who wanted an internship. Martino helped Kimmel land one at Rutgers through OSHEP. "I told him to go out and see what he could find out about those people lined up on the street and that could be his internship," Martino said.

A few months later, Kimmel "wrote like a twenty-page paper on it—this very Marxist-laden document that probably didn't have a lot of use in that regard," Martino recalled. "But that's where we learned that they were temp workers and people coming from Mexico."

Their next move was to arrange for Rutgers to pay Kimmel a modest stipend for research and put him "out on the street as a salt," Martino said. *Salt* is an old union term, defined as someone who takes a job for another purpose than simply earning a paycheck. For unions, that purpose is usually organizing the other employees into a union.

That was Martino and Cunningham's intent, although maybe not exactly a union, maybe something different, but something that would empower workers to change their lives.

A lofty idea, and to accomplish it, Kimmel, by then a college graduate, spent his first eighteen post-diploma months working for temporary staffing agencies, loading and unloading trucks, tightening bottle caps, and producing bleach. On his first day on the job, he failed at his first assignment. He couldn't keep up the pace. Soon, though, he learned how to handle the workload.

"You have to figure out how to do it in the most efficient way," Kimmel said. "I never came in assuming I knew anything. Little by little you learn the rhythm." Asking for advice was a way to make a connection—and improve his Spanish. In a car parts warehouse, he'd have to crawl from the top rack of one set of shelves to the top rack of another. If Kimmel had fallen in the gaps between the racks, it would have been a long way to the floor.

"We had some random jobs. A contractor hired us to de-weed a pond. We were given boots and had to pull the weeds out," he said. "At Sony, we had to line up the televisions and stereos in a line, so the forklifts could move them."

One job involved quality control, twisting bottle tops to make sure they were on tightly.

"I woke up in the middle of the night twisting my girlfriend's shoulder," he said.

On the job, Kimmel experienced many of the problems common to temp workers. "In the bleach factory, there was no eye protection," he said. Often, he'd travel to jobs in an overcrowded van, perched on a wheel well, or because he's slender, sitting on an overturned crate in the front between the driver and the front passenger. "Sometimes we'd get abandoned at work and would have to walk or try to get rides from other workers."

Like others who worked as temps or as *jornaleros en la esquina* (workers hired from the corner), Kimmel became a victim of wage theft. For several weeks in a row, Kimmel received checks totaling $628. Each bounced. Every Friday, the local manager promised to make good, but several Fridays passed, and nothing changed. Luckily for him, Kimmel wasn't completely relying on his temp worker wages, since he had the modest Rutgers stipend. Also, he had the know-how to press the agency's corporate headquarters to make good on the bounced checks, eventually recovering the money.

Kimmel later learned another wage theft tactic: some agencies will try to avoid paying wages by drafting paychecks, but then finding excuses not to deliver them to the workers. They hope the workers, frustrated, will give up. If they do, in ninety days the checks become invalid and can't be cashed.

In 1999 and 2000, with Kimmel reporting from the frontlines, Martino and Cunningham entertained hopes that the workers might want an uprising, or to form a union, or to protest, or something exciting, something worth organizing. They were disappointed. What Kimmel had learned on the job, at weekend soccer games or at parties, was simple. The workers wanted to learn English.

"We were just trying to figure it all out," Kimmel said. "I wasn't going to blow my cover. Every now and then, someone would talk about a union, but those people were few and far between." Eventually, tired of hearing Kimmel report on English classes, Martino and Cunningham told Kimmel to teach one, mainly to shut him up. Never mind that Kimmel had no idea how to teach someone English. "We said, 'Well, learn. You'll figure it out.'" Martino recalled.

"And that's what he did, and that's how New Labor got its start."

Kimmel said they had "wanted to start as a temp worker organization, but it didn't turn out." What turned out was an English learning and computer literacy group. But it was always about organizing through education and the Small Group Activity Method.

Despite New Labor's proximity to Rutgers University in New Brunswick, residents of the poorest neighborhoods in the city needed access to computers and English language classes.

The jobs available to them were low-wage ones: housecleaning, office cleaning, landscaping, dishwashing and cooking in restaurants, non-union construction, hotel housekeeping, factory work, and child care. The center provided a safe space for immigrant workers to talk about their jobs. The discussion topics, both in casual conversations and those on the agenda for scheduled meetings, were familiar to most low-wage workers—unpredictable schedules, lack of training, safety concerns, sexual harassment— but compounded by language differences, discrimination, and immigration status vulnerability.

Martino landed a job at Rutgers. For a while, he and OSHEP Rutgers administrator Debra Lancaster were able to string enough money together, usually from worker safety grants, to keep Kimmel and Cunningham employed. Sometimes funding ran out and they became unemployed, working at the center as volunteers.

In 2002, New Labor almost shut down, but a grant from the federal Occupational Safety and Health Administration (OSHA) saved the organization, providing money for another round of worker safety training. OSHA's Susan Harwood Training Grant program provides funding to nonprofit organizations for worker health and safety education and training. Recipients of the funding are tasked to deliver their programs to small businesses and to workers who are hard to reach, have limited English proficiency, or who work in high-hazard industries.

Kimmel and Cunningham continued their trainings at New Labor, while Kimmel also went to the corners to mobilize day laborers and temp workers. In 2009, Cunningham, thirty-two, died of colon cancer.

From 2004 to 2007, Kimmel regularly traveled to corners in
Newark, Lakewood, Red Bank, Orange, Dover, and New Brunswick. Dynamics were challenging. At one corner, the owner
of a convenience store didn't like the gathering of *jornaleros* on
the sidewalk near the store; but he liked selling them coffee and
snacks.

"You get there at 6 a.m. or 7 a.m.," Kimmel said. "Eventually,
you learn the times to go to each corner. The biggest problem is
turnover. You go there one day, and if you go there the next day,
nobody knows you." Because he is white, Kimmel said he had to
work extra hard to earn the workers' trust. "I'd bring pictures and
show previous trainings. If a contractor would show up, people
would run away."

Around the state, churches and synagogues often provided
initial meeting spaces. In Lakewood, for example, day laborers
convened in a local church and in New Brunswick, Anshe Emeth
Memorial Temple, a synagogue, hosts the annual Worker Memorial Day ceremony. In New Brunswick, New Labor partnered
with Unity Square, a Catholic Charities–supported neighborhood revitalization and social services group in one of the city's
immigrant communities.

In 2013, "we went door to door in a four-block square area and
discovered that 16 to 17 percent of the people had suffered wage
theft in the past six months," Kimmel said. That survey, with support from Unity Square, led to the passage of the wage theft law
later in the year.

Throughout its history, New Labor has never lost a focus on
health and safety.

Key to New Labor's efforts is its reliance on the Small Group
Activity Method training model. In April 2019, restaurant workers gathered for training, climbing up a steep flight of stairs to
reach New Labor's second-floor headquarters above a law office in
New Brunswick.

The workers talked about slipping and falling on wet kitchen floors, being struck by the door to the kitchen opening and closing, tripping over door stops, and about being burned by hot pots, pans, and trays. Following a group activity, they talked about how those hazards could be remedied. Then they practiced talking to their bosses about the conditions.

The same thinking applies to training about hazards on construction sites or in factories. If workers become aware of the hazards and learn what should be done to correct them, they might have the courage, whatever their immigration status, to speak up to the boss.

"This group helped me to learn English and helped me to fight about my rights," said Edwin Vasquez, of New Brunswick, one of the workers who attended a session in April 2019.

"New Labor is like a second home for me," said Alberto Jandete, of New Brunswick, who works in a factory that manufactures cosmetics. "I'm no more scared on my job. I know my rights. Everything, everything is safety."

New Labor developed a "safety liaison" program where workers who completed enough training to gain expertise in safety and in negotiating with their supervisors kept tabs on their own workplaces. The program grew into its own in the demolition and rebuilding boom that followed the devastation inflicted by Hurricane Sandy along New Jersey's Atlantic coast in 2012. Safety liaisons visited affected areas, handing out personal protective equipment and providing on-the-spot trainings.

In 2014, some of New Labor's safety liaison members became OSHA-authorized safety and health trainers. As their knowledge grew, so did their status as safety experts in their communities and on their jobsites. In many cases, employers also relied on the liaisons' expertise, knowing the liaisons couldn't be ignored because of the credibility they had built with OSHA. The liaisons knew exactly when to negotiate, when to stop the work, and when to call their contacts at OSHA. The liaisons had expertise, confidence, and connections.

Ironically, the safety training dollars that had kept the organization afloat in its early days were posing a challenge in the spring of 2019.

In 2017, New York City passed a law requiring construction workers to have received "OSHA 10" training within the last five years.[1] By December 1, 2019, workers at most major construction sites were required to have completed thirty hours of safety training from an authorized instructor. New Labor, because of its proximity to New York City, is known as a place that can provide it.

"There's a huge demand for the training, high demand," Kimmel said. "People come in and they may even think we are OSHA."

"If we're just a training center, we're not building power," he said. "It's not just training that matters. If the boss tells you do something, you might still do it. It's how to evaluate: Is my life at risk? How do we approach the boss about it? How do we talk to workers? How do we make the hard decision to reject the work?

"There's job fear," Kimmel said. "For example, you have a day laborer who needs the work and has to send money home to his family. That's especially true in the winter, when jobs are harder to come by. They say, 'I'll take the job. I hope for the best. It's just one day.' But it could be the last day. They say, 'I have to risk myself. I don't have any rights.' But we teach them that you do have rights. Workers have to learn to [confront their bosses about safety] on their own, because construction sites are dynamic," Kimmel said.

They can't always rely on advocates such as New Labor or OSHA for help.

"Conditions are always changing. In New Jersey, the OSHA offices are far away. Just because you call OSHA doesn't mean they'll come right away. Even if they do, they often have an hour ride, and conditions can change."

At the Worker Memorial Day service on April 28, 2019, an OSHA official commended Kimmel for drawing the agency's attention to hazardous workplaces. Martino was in the audience and applauded as well.

As well known as New Labor has become as a worker center, the search for the best form of worker empowerment has not come to an end—not for Kimmel, not for Martino.

Martino thinks about the potential for New Labor to organize a community union—a union based on people who live in the same area. "When you look at this workforce, on the one hand, they're very alienated in their work on a daily basis. But, at the same time, what they have is that they all get shipped back to their community every day. Unlike the rest of us, low-wage workers, who are still primarily immigrants in New Jersey, live in communities that look like company towns."

Martino's vision is for workers in those communities to set the floor for employment—and employers, needing the labor, would have no choice but to agree. "I think it's worth pointing out," he said, "that most of the organizations that became worker centers weren't founded by people with previous union experience," unlike New Labor, which had union leaders like Martino at the start.

"So, they came at it from a very different point of view," he said.

"We were trying to help people move up the job ladder, if you will, by knowing English," he said. "So, to that extent, we look more like a union-driven organization than other centers. And we had paying members, which again is driven by our union experience.

"We wanted to figure out how to do a union that made sense to the worker and made sense to the employers. That was the plan, or that was the hope. That was the vision," Martino said.

Before the term was fostered and explained by Rutgers University professor Janice Fine, "we never thought of ourselves as a worker center," Martino said. "We are still in pursuit of this new version of a union.

"New Labor," he said. "Exactly."

Fatuma Abib, member, Greater Minnesota Worker Center, St. Cloud. *I. George Bilyk*

Shelly Ruzicka, communications director, Arise Chicago. *Jane M. Von Bergen*

Part III

Friends and Allies

When it comes to making real change in the workplace, workers, ultimately, must be the ones to use their voices and build their power. But they find allies in other places, particularly among academics and people of faith. These partners lend expertise, credibility, and, often, opportunities for funding. Don't, however, get the impression that it's a one-way street, with the educated elite charitably bestowing their assistance in a kind of misplaced noblesse oblige. Quite the contrary.

Our founding sounds like the start of a bad joke: A rabbi, a monsignor, a Methodist bishop, and an organizer founded Arise Chicago.

—Shelly Ruzicka, Arise Chicago

The way I think of public sociology is to get involved in actions. . . . Movements live and die with support, support from the public, especially movements of the poor.

—Professor Stephen E. Philion,
St. Cloud State University,
Greater Minnesota Worker Center

10

PULPITS AND PROFESSORS

I n St. Cloud, Minnesota, winter comes early.
It was already freezing cold when eighty demonstrators—
Somali poultry workers, community activists, a handful of college
students and their professor—protested outside a St. Cloud temp
agency in November 2014. They complained the agency was abusing Somali workers by channeling them to the lowest-paying jobs
at the nearby Gold'n Plump poultry plant and firing them without explanation.

Signs and shouts may have been a new experience for the
St. Cloud State University students, but not for their professor.
Sociologist Stephen E. Philion refuses to just *think* about societies.
Instead, he describes himself as a "public sociologist." Philion explained: "The way I think of public sociology is to get involved in
actions. . . . Movements live and die with support, support from
the public, especially movements of the poor." [1]

In Chicago, the clergy were mystified. They manned their mission kitchens, dishing chicken noodle soup to the poor, only to
discover that many of the poor had jobs, but still couldn't make
ends meet. Why, the clergy wondered, "if they have a job, are they
coming to a soup kitchen?" said Shelly Ruzicka, communications
director at Arise Chicago, a community labor organization led by
a minister. "That's just not right. If you have a job, you should be
able to support a family."

And it was at that junction of charity and challenge that Kim
Bobo stepped in. Bobo calls herself a faith organizer. "I think that

people get that doing soup kitchens and shelters is not enough," she explained in an interview with historian Joseph McCartin.[2] What people lacked was a practical way to tackle the bigger structural problems. For more than forty years, Bobo has been promoting concrete activities for religious communities to confront the root of injustice.

The work done by academics like Philion and faith leaders like Bobo may be worlds away from the grueling struggle in poultry plants, the exhausting tedium in warehouses, the perilous danger on construction sites, and the draining isolation of housecleaning, but Philion and Bobo represent key allies in the worker center movement.

For the worker centers, academics provide needed research—designing surveys and studies that become the basis of campaigns for better wages and working conditions. They develop trainings that build capability. Faith communities add a layer of morality to struggles that may seem purely economic. Both academic and faith partners offer credibility and bridges to the wider community, sources of funding and support. Importantly, both can mobilize constituencies—students, fellow academics, worshippers—multiplying the effectiveness of advocacy.

But it would be a mistake to see this relationship as a one-way street. It's not just the privileged elite reaching down, or out, to extend a hand to the marginalized.

The relationship is reciprocal. Religions call on believers to live out their faith, with action giving meaning to prayer. Being a moral voice in the community matters. Likewise, some academic disciplines depend on social engagement, so their work is grounded in community needs. Their research endeavors, which are tied to career advancement, must be relevant to a public need and capable of demonstrating an impact.

Arise Chicago's Ruzicka says, "Our founding sounds like the start of a bad joke: a rabbi, a monsignor, a Methodist bishop, and an organizer founded Arise Chicago." It's true that Arise's precursor organization was actually an alliance of labor and religious leaders. It was the early 1990s.

Bobo, the organizer behind that alliance, was a significant figure in the history of worker centers. "The work of engaging the religious community in labor issues is nothing new," Bobo told the historian McCartin. "We are building on much history in both the religious and labor communities that went before us."[3]

Bobo is part of that history. In 1989, Bobo pulled together a network of religious leaders to support nineteen hundred striking coal miners in Kentucky, Virginia, and West Virginia. Many traveled to the picket line and strike headquarters. Bobo organized delegations of the faith leaders to meet with the Pittston Coal Company's board of directors.

The United Mine Workers Union strike lasted ten months and provoked wildcat strikes by more than forty thousand angry U.S. coal miners elsewhere. The experience reinforced Bobo's instinct that there was great potential for organizing people of faith on worker injustice.

In 1991, an alliance of labor and religious leaders became the Chicago Interfaith Committee on Worker Issues. The idea was "to raise the moral voice and organize different faith communities to support labor union members," said Adam Kader, director of Arise Chicago Worker Center. Arise Chicago grew from the Chicago Interfaith Committee.

"Union members go on strike and so we will do collections across congregations for the families of striking workers. A boss is negotiating in bad faith with the union and so we'll send a delegation of clergy members to pressure that employer to negotiate in good faith. Things like that," he said. "That's how we were designed as an organization."

Unions outside of Chicago were witnessing the way that faith leaders were validating workers' struggles. They saw the influence that the religious community had with employers. Unions wanted more of it. The Interfaith Committee on Worker Issues grew its network, and in 1996 Bobo founded the National Interfaith Committee on Worker Justice, shortened later to Interfaith Worker Justice (IWJ).[4]

The organization's prominence grew, and as Bobo explained, pastors started referring workers to the committee because they were having problems at work, in particular not getting paid.

"When we tried simply referring the workers to unions, we quickly learned that many of the workers came from shops that were too small for unions to organize or from sectors where no unions were focusing," Bobo said. "In the early days, I remember losing many days of work trying to help these poor workers with horrible situations."[5]

IWJ created a workers' rights manual, with versions in English, Spanish, and Polish, and distributed it through its network of churches. It was 2001 and Kader, who'd studied the history of Arise Chicago, described it as a turning point. "Suddenly all these workers that didn't belong to labor unions but who were being screwed on the job contacted us saying, 'I got your workers' rights book. I'm not being paid. I'm being discriminated against. I'm being sexually harassed. There's a health and safety hazard. What do I do?' And the organization was like, 'Yeah, what do you?' So the organization said, 'Let's start a program to deal with all these workers that don't belong to labor unions.' And that was the idea for the worker center.

"It would be a place where non-union workers could come and get resources to defend themselves," he said. At first, the worker center "was more of a social service, because it was in response to a community need. 'Come in, we're going to help you.'"

Helping people, Kader said, fit in with a religious sensibility. "We were meeting workers where they were at. They said they needed help and we were giving them help."

When Kader joined the center in December 2006, he saw a problem, however, with simply giving help. "There were hundreds of workers coming to our doors and we were handing them a form to fill out to send to the Department of Labor and then we say goodbye to them and they leave. Or, workers are raising important problems and we're referring them to an attorney, who is going to sue the company and make a lot of money on that case.

"We're bleeding potential power. There are all these people here that we could be doing things with," he said. "I saw this as a potential vehicle for social change."

Religious organizations have always been interested in charity. "It's that soup kitchen kind of thing," Kader acknowledged. "However, with this organization, we were able to engage a lot of congregations in things that were more oriented towards power building."

Arise Chicago's roots embody "the parallel work of all the clergy organizing for labor unions, which still continues to this day, which is very strong," Kader said. "And I think it was a strong program at the time, too."

Just as the Chicago Interfaith Committee on Worker Issues laid the foundation for the national organization Interfaith Worker Justice, IWJ planted the seeds for worker centers and affiliated groups nationwide. By 2009, IWJ had a staff of twenty and was providing financial and technical support to worker centers in twelve states.[6]

In Syracuse, New York, for example, the Central New York Labor-Religion Coalition was looking for a project that would address economic injustice in its community. Its leaders were inspired to establish a worker center following visits in 2005 by two individuals: Jose Oliva, who was IWJ's worker center network coordinator,[7] and Janice Fine, who was an assistant professor at Rutgers University and is considered a leading expert on the worker center movement.[8]

The Workers' Center of Central New York (WCCNY) in Syracuse opened its doors in 2006. Gretchen Purser, chair of the WCCNY executive board, noted the religious community's support for the organization. The center receives considerable financial support from the Catholic Campaign for Human Development (CCHD), a source of funding for other worker centers across the country.

CCHD is currently the center's biggest contributor. Purser explained that CCHD is interested in funding organizations "that organize the poor; that's their mission." It seems like they couldn't find a better match, recognizing the economic vulnerability of immigrant farmworkers, who make up the core membership of the Workers' Center of Central New York.

"Yes, there are some strings attached to CCHD funding," Purser said, describing it as a "challenge." "We can't lobby for abortion rights or LGBT rights or anything like that, not that our organization would, because it's not part of our mission." The CCHD has also been a longtime source of funding for the Latino Union of Chicago, said Analía Rodríguez, the worker center's executive director. "We always have had connections with the faith community. There has always been support. There has always been interest. There is also a Catholic university that we partner up with," she said.

The service aspect of the Latino Union is a draw for religious organizations.

"They've come through with volunteer hours. They've come through with money. They've come through with helpful exposure," Rodríguez said. "They've also been a venue for us when we go to specific places to talk. We had a huge collaboration with a group of synagogues and the Jewish community to talk about what we were doing with the Domestic Worker Bill of Rights."

She notes that churches can provide another venue to communicate with businesspeople who are members of their congregations. "If you're an employer, then there's that avenue for us to be able to go and talk to you and share the experience of the worker side." Moreover, because the Latino Union of Chicago has a hiring hall, Rodríguez explains, gatherings with faith communities represent potential employers for their members. "Everywhere we go we always talk about the hiring hall. Every presentation we do, every tabling, everything, we always mention the hiring hall."

The religious community's support of worker centers also can take a more public face. It continues the tradition of U.S. faith leaders who add their moral voice to worker campaigns for justice. There are the high-profile instances, such as Rev. Dr. Martin Luther King Jr.'s efforts on behalf of striking sanitation workers in Memphis, the delegations of religious leaders who joined the picket lines in 1989 with United Mine Workers during their strike against the Pittston Coal Company, and the fifty religious groups who organized the forty-day "Fast from Fast Food" in 2015 to support the nationwide "Fight for $15" minimum wage campaign.

Lesser-known events are equally meaningful. In October 2018, when twenty diaper-wearing demonstrators lined the driveway of a poultry plant in Bryan, Texas, Rev. Trent Williams stood with them. They held homemade signs that read: "Let My People Pee" and "Love the Workers as You Love the Chickens."

Centro de Derechos Laborales (CDL), a worker center established by the Brazos County Interfaith Immigration Network, organized the event outside of the Sanderson Farms plant. CDL wanted to draw public attention to issues inside the plant—harsh chemicals, sexual harassment, and lack of access to the bathroom.

Rev. Williams, associate pastor with the Friends Congregational Church, stood with the demonstrators. Speaking in front of the camera for the local television station, he called on all companies to treat their employees with dignity and respect. CDL chose Rev. Williams to be one of four people to carry a message detailing complaints to Sanderson's CEO, handing it personally to the plant manager. Having Rev. Williams at the demonstration meant a lot, said demonstrator Hortensia Bustos, who previously worked at the plant and knew people inside would be afraid to speak up. "We felt supported, safe, and more confident with the

Reverend present," she said, speaking in Spanish through a translator. "It is so nice that in situations like this they support us."

Professor Philion often finds himself at labor and immigrant rights demonstrations in the Minneapolis–St. Paul region. He's a familiar face. Over the years, his sociology students at St. Cloud State University have asked him what he does at the protests.

"You show up. You show support," he answers. "You're not an academic, you're not a worker, you're just a body. You show support."[9] He challenges his colleagues and students to promote and get involved in civil actions—to be more than a disinterested observer or a bystander. It's what Philion means when he calls himself a "public sociologist."

Early in his academic career, Philion assembled a network of academics in the Twin Cities who could mobilize at a moment's notice to show support at picket lines or working-class protests. When immigrant rights marches took over U.S. cities in 2006, the network joined those, too. The struggle for labor rights falls hardest on immigrants because they are particularly vulnerable to employer abuse and discrimination.

The Twin Cities are home to more Somali immigrants than any other U.S. city. Philion spent a career studying immigrants and their experiences. He wanted to do more to help the Somali immigrants who settled in Minnesota, "but he didn't have the connections," explained Ahmed Ali, former executive director of the Greater Minnesota Worker Center (GMWC) in St. Cloud and a Somali immigrant.

GMWC started in 2013 as an all-volunteer organization, cofounded primarily by Ali and Philion. "We got together in the community and talked about putting together a worker center," Philion explained. It would be a place "that trains workers on how to organize in the workplace where they don't have a union, and especially for low-wage workers. We knew there were models down in the Cities to borrow from, models from around the country to borrow from," he said.[10]

The vision is a center where immigrant and low-wage workers can become empowered. If the question posed by a worker was "What can you do for me?" Philion's answer was: "We can't do anything *for* you, but we can help you train yourself how to organize, and train others to organize, and go right to the workplace and demand change. We'll be backing you."

A pivotal moment for the young, volunteer organization was that freezing cold day in November 2014 outside the St. Cloud temp agency abusing Somali workers by channeling them to the lowest-paying jobs at the Gold'n Plump poultry plant. Having eighty people, including Philion, show up in the cold demonstrated the power of organizing. It tapped into the community's anger about workplace labor abuses—not just among Somali workers, but also in the community at large.

The event fortified GMWC's volunteers and membership. By 2015, the worker center had a $200,000 budget and Ahmed Ali was the executive director. The St. Cloud State University professor continues to serve on the center's board of directors. Philion is steadfast in his challenge to colleagues and students "to get involved in actions that challenge the capitalist hegemonic way of thinking and acting." [11]

The headline on Arkansas Public Radio was "Study Finds Worker Abuse in Arkansas Poultry Industry." At the *Arkansas Times* it read, "Study Slams Arkansas Poultry Processing Plants for Low Wages, Lack of Sick Leave." [12]

The media accounts in February 2016 were based on collaborative research by the Northwest Arkansas Workers' Justice Center (NWAWJC), sociologist Chris Brenner at the University of California, Santa Cruz, and the Food Labor Research Center at the University of California, Berkeley. NWAWJC's membership works primarily in the region's poultry plants. They are experts on the low wages and unsafe conditions. They had stories and experiences to share.[13]

But stories only go so far and may not lead to change. NWAWJC members wanted their reality to be more influential. They knew that collaborating with academic researchers to conduct a study of working conditions in one of the state's leading industries would help their cause. It would make the hardships that they, as poultry workers, experienced more credible to legislators and policymakers.

The collaboration produced *Wages and Working Conditions in Arkansas Poultry Plants*.[14] The forty-eight-page report included findings from a survey of five hundred poultry processing workers from ten different companies operating in the state. The researchers noted that although the population of Arkansas is 79 percent white, workers in the state's poultry processing plants are primarily people of color. The survey reflected this disparity, with 46 percent of respondents identifying as Latino, and another 41 percent as Black or Asian-Pacific Islanders.

The researchers learned workers felt intense production pressure, with 54 percent reporting that the fast pace forced them to do things that might harm consumers. Sixty-two percent of the laborers worked when sick. Only 9 percent reported having paid sick leave. Workers also reported a perverse "point system" that compelled them to go to work sick.

The researchers conducted in-depth interviews with thirty workers. They heard about restrictions on going to the restroom when nature called. The restrooms could be far away, but workers were allotted only ten minutes to relieve themselves. "By the time you remove your gear, and return to your position, you have gone over the time allowed," one worker explained during her interview.

Some workers reported getting "points" on their record for taking too long in the bathroom. The women who talked about this issue considered it gender discrimination. Male supervisors failed to acknowledge that women need to use the bathroom more frequently, including when menstruating or pregnant. NWAWJC was strategic about when to release the report, timing it to coincide with Tyson Foods' annual shareholders' meeting in Springdale, Arkansas, its headquarters. Tyson Foods, Inc., the biggest poultry company in the United States, produced 38 million broiler chickens *per week* in 2019.[15]

When investors arrived at the Northwest Arkansas Convention Center they had to pass a sidewalk lined with protesters, holding aloft signs calling for dignity, respect, better wages, and better conditions for poultry workers. The protestors distributed leaflets with a link to the report and made sure a Tyson official had a copy. The demonstrators were members of the worker center, accompanied by the Unitarian Universalist Service Committee—an example of a triumvirate collaboration of worker centers with their faith and academic partners.

Tyson Foods wanted to be talking about its stronger financial outlook, but, because of the report, was forced to respond to press inquiries about bathroom breaks and sick leave. The company produced a written statement: "We wouldn't be a successful company without our Team Members. We care about them and we're continually working to make sure they're treated fairly."[16]

The results of NWAWJC's collaboration with the university researchers attracted the attention the worker center wanted. The press noticed and the poultry industry noticed, with ramifications for the industry and its workers beyond Arkansas poultry production.

Tyson made a public commitment to upgrading workplace safety and health, worker representation, and wages. It came because of NWAWJC's pressure and a parallel effort by Oxfam America—an ally of the worker center—to compel Tyson to raise the bar on labor standards and set an example for the rest of the industry.

But such reports serve other purposes for worker centers, particularly helping with fundraising and organizing.

"Foundations," explained Kader, director of Arise Chicago Worker Center, "when they are researching issues and deciding priorities for their funding portfolios and who to fund, will consult with the research. They'll do a literature review. They'll see what the literature says about this."

The academic research, Kader added, means "our issues are being considered. It's influencing the conversation at the policy level and influencing conversation at the funding level."

For example, researchers at the University of Illinois at Chicago (UIC) conducted an influential study on wage theft—a pressing problem for low-wage workers when employers short them on pay. Arise Chicago was one of the community partners that advised on design of the study, conducted surveys, provided translation, and contributed expertise to drafts of the report.[17] Although the wage theft report was published in 2009, it continues to be cited by academics, worker centers, and other labor allies because of its seminal research. Research from the study has been used to influence anti–wage theft legislation around the country.

"The UIC study we quote all the time because it is a really tangible way for people to understand—a million dollars a day in wage theft," said Kader's colleague, Shelly Ruzicka, director of communication. As a worker center, "we would never have the capacity to do that kind of research."

Kader is on the advisory committee for the Labor Research Action Network. It "brings together researchers and practitioners, unionists, worker center activists, union researchers, university researchers," Kader said. "The idea is how research is influencing organizing and how the organizing is influencing research," he said. "It's a virtuous cycle."

The cycle has been repeated around the country.

In upstate New York, Gretchen Purser, associate sociology professor at Syracuse University, penned *Milked: Immigrant Dairy*

Farmworkers in New York State. Purser, board chair of the Workers' Center of Central New York, worked in collaboration with activists and workers from her center, as well as representatives of the Worker Justice Center of New York.[18]

The 2017 report detailed the brutal conditions and overwork done mostly by immigrants on dairy farms in the New York countryside. Some workers milk cows in four-hour shifts, with no time to catch up on sleep. Cows and calves kick workers, but there's no help. Workers fall on wet or frozen silage. Conditions are cold and wet, and the farms are isolated, with workers sometimes living in below-standard housing.

In Los Angeles, the Garment Worker Center teamed up with the Center for Labor Research and Education and Labor Occupational Safety and Health, both at the University of California, Los Angeles, to produce a thirty-two-page report, *Dirty Threads, Dangerous Factories: Health and Safety in Los Angeles' Fashion Industry*, in 2016.[19]

Sewing machine operators typically sit for eight to ten hours on hard metal folding chairs, hunched over their equipment, repeating the same movements with shoulders, arms, and hands hundreds of times a day, the report noted. Pressers and trimmers stand all day handling hundreds of pieces of fabric. More than 70 percent of the workers said their factories were brimming with dust. Some sewed together scraps of fabric to make dust masks. Many reported infestations of rats, mice, and cockroaches, sweltering heat, and poor lighting. They worried about blocked exits and overstocked workspaces that impeded their movement.

In El Paso, Texas, the Fuerza del Valle Workers' Center collaborated with other advocacy groups and academics to produce *Living in the Shadows: Latina Domestic Workers in the Texas-Mexico Border Region*, a thirty-two-page report released in 2018 by the National Domestic Workers Alliance.[20]

More than a third of the 516 workers surveyed couldn't earn enough to fend off hunger. One in four domestic workers—nannies, housekeepers, and people who care for the elderly or disabled—experienced wage theft, and 12 percent reported being pushed or physically hurt by their employer or someone in their employer's home. Live-in workers were particularly vulnerable, with 45 percent experiencing wage theft, 31 percent reporting being pushed or physically hurt, and 45 percent being injured on the job.

In all three cases, the reports have contributed to momentum leading to changes in policy or legislation. In New York, for example, dairy workers won the right to be covered by the state's version of the U.S. Fair Labor Standards Act. With that, they must now be paid minimum wage and overtime, plus be allowed to form unions, if they wish.

"Research when done well can be a form of an organizing tool," said Adam Kader, director of Arise Chicago Worker Center. "It's a way to recruit new members and strengthen the organization."

In Chicago, domestic workers were drawn to Arise Chicago's trainings in green cleaning—the use of environmentally safe cleaning chemicals that are also safe for workers and their customers. Those trainings were developed by Joseph Zanoni, a faculty member at the University of Illinois at Chicago (UIC) School of Public Health, and Marsha Love, a program manager at UIC's Center for Healthy Work. Zanoni sits on the board at the Latino Union, which also offers the training.

Housekeepers come for the training, but at Arise Chicago, staffer Ania Jakubek, who organizes Polish domestic workers, makes sure they get at least forty-five solid minutes of worker rights. "On the end is always a semi-organizing drive," she said.

What may matter most in the reports is the way the underlying surveys contribute to organizing. Whether it was 516 domestic workers on the Tex-Mex border, 307 garment workers in Los Angeles, or 88 immigrant dairy workers on 53 farms in upstate New York, the surveys gave workers who had no voice a chance to share stories about their struggles. Through the surveys, contacts are made and materials are distributed.

"We did qualitative research, just listening to their stories for an hour or two," said Carly Fox, formerly with the Worker Justice Center of New York. "It was a 240-question survey. All of them said that none of them had anyone to listen to them. Eighty-eight people got their story told.

"It's an old narrative that they have no voice," she said. "We're trying to negate that paradigm."

11

A TIME TO PRAY

Almost imperceptibly it began, first as a small murmur, then just a little louder, indistinguishable from the earlier, hushed bedside conversations in Somali, the sound of a language mostly unknown to Americans. But then, as the dozen men spoke, their hands raised elbow height, palms up, the sounds coalesced into prayer—a prayer to Allah for healing.

The man in the hospital bed, small and frightened, needed the prayers. The night before, while working at the Jennie-O turkey processing factory in Melrose, near St. Cloud, Minnesota, he had been crushed against the wall by a forklift. His left hip and leg were shattered and there were injuries to his bladder. A nurse came by with a pain pill.

"He is fighting for his life," said Ahmed Ali, then executive director of the Greater Minnesota Worker Center (GMWC) and now on its board. GMWC has been pushing for safety improvements and break times for workers at that processing factory and other plants for more than five years.

Along with safety, prayer breaks for the Muslim workforce is a key issue. Protests and rallies had won accommodations, but there was more to be done.

"If I had to choose between prayer and work, I'd choose prayer," said Fatuma Abib, in her forties, a worker center member who had been a Jennie-O employee. She was among those who had contacted Ali with the news about the worker, who was injured on

August 9, 2019. Ali had spent part of the next day trying to discover the worker's identity and whereabouts.

For Ali—and for the man—the information was critical. What workers have told Ali is that an injury at the plant in Melrose will usually lead to a firing—maybe not immediately, but over time. Workers have told him that the company will shift the blame for accidents, deserved or not, to injured workers and force them, through assignments their bodies can no longer handle, to quit. If not, they can be fired for not keeping up with production, the workers said.

Sometimes Ali can help. Maybe he can't save the job, but he can, perhaps, connect the worker with lawyers and doctors so at least, through workers' compensation, medical bills can be covered. That's what the GMWC did for the man who was lying in the hospital bed. He had yet to return to work as of November 2019 and may be paralyzed.

Helping the man would, of course, help the man. But every benefit for any worker and for St. Cloud's Somali workers as a group means more strength to the GMWC. Ali started the worker center in 2013 with Stephen E. Philion, a sociology professor at St. Cloud State University, and others. Philion's research on immigrant workers in the United States, particularly Somali immigrants in Minnesota, led him to activism.

Philion "wanted to do more, but he didn't have the connections," Ali said.

In the United States, many worker centers focus on Latino workers, but in Minnesota, Somali immigrants change both the dynamics and some of the issues—not only for the worker centers, but for the surrounding community.

The highway strip outside St. Cloud where GMWC has its office is distinctly unappealing. Worn-out shopping centers and faded one-story office buildings badly need paint, and pockmarked parking lots cry out for resurfacing. Even so, cars jockey for space at the nearby Star City Mall. It's not much of a mall, more like a strip shopping center that has seen better times. But the parking lot is packed with shoppers heading to an African grocery, a Somali restaurant, and other Somali-owned businesses. Nearby is a Somali-owned coffee shop. Owners of daycare centers and restaurants, Somali immigrants are rehabbing former schools and tired apartment buildings.

"Ten years ago, this mall was empty," Ali said, threading his car through the lot. "Now it's full."

To understand the workers, it's important to understand their past.

Many came to St. Cloud from refugee camps like Dadaab in Kenya, a "city" of half a million, where some, fleeing from violence in Somalia, had lived for decades. When Ali came to the United States in 2006, he had spent more than half his life—fifteen years—in the camp.

Jobs in Minnesota's meat processing plants drew them to the state—they could eviscerate chickens without being able to speak English. Over time, families coalesced and a community grew, with more coming through government resettlement contracts.

What Minnesota's Somalis share with all workers is vulnerability to losing work, rough conditions, and wage theft. But there is a key difference between them and many Latino members of worker centers across the United States. The Somali immigrants don't face the threat of being rounded up and deported.

"Almost 99.99 percent are legal," Ali said. "So they are not afraid of that kind of retaliation.

"The strongest voices we have are the single moms. They are the breadwinners in their families, and they are speaking to the media and putting their faces in print and online and in broadcast media. These are workers you think would be vulnerable, because if they get fired, they lose the basis of their livelihoods, but they are not afraid.

"The only challenge is that it takes us time to prepare these workers for leadership roles. Because they are coming from countries that, in the case of Somalia, had years of military dictatorship, they had not had the opportunities for union organizing," he said.

"And those who were in Ethiopia—Ethiopia is a very repressive regime. Whatever the government says, you can't lift up your head and say no. So it takes us time to integrate them and say, 'Hey, this is a different country. You have freedom of speech and you can actually fight on the issues.' Once they realize the power they have, there is no stopping them."

Ali described Somalia as a freedom-loving country with an egalitarian society that moved from British and Italian rule to democracy before a military dictatorship seized control. Civil war ensued, with factions also manipulated as proxies in the Cold War between the United States and the former Soviet Republic. "It became more tribal, more divided, more regional," Ali said, as groups tried to solidify power in the chaos.

Many people fled to refugee camps. Ali's father was killed in the fighting.

"What they have to overcome is that they came in with a fighting spirit," Ali said. "That's really good, but the whole union thing is new to them. You have to educate them," because they are accustomed to factionalism and relying on themselves for survival. If they are unhappy at work, for example, Ali must urge them not to quit, "because that's not going to solve the issues. Other workers will have to stay and face the challenges."

Many, he said, "have experienced chaos and the brute force of violence and power. It creates a fear of authority. And so, before we put them into actions, we have to provide them trainings: 'Here is what the law says. You have rights.'"

Some trainings involve issues common to poultry processing workers—bathroom breaks and injuries from line speed.

"You have to be allowed to use the restroom when you need it— not just during breaks, not when the manager thinks you should go to use the restroom. If your body says you need to use the rest-room, you need to use the restroom," Ali said he tells workers.

"We hear stories of people peeing on the line because no one will let them go to the bathroom, or of workers saying, 'I don't drink water because I know my supervisor is not going to let me use the bathroom,' so they become dehydrated," Ali said. "We hear workers say they wear diapers to work. We tell them you have a right to use the restroom when you need it."

Fatuma Abib can talk about the injuries. Stepping down from a platform, she caught her hand in a machine in December 2017.

"It's unusual that I survived with my fingers because the people who got their hand caught in that machine before, their fingers came off," she said, as Ali translated. "I was lucky I had several lay-ers of safety gloves. That's how my hand got saved. Otherwise my fingers would have come off my hand."

To extricate her hand, mechanics had to disassemble the ma-chine. She went to the hospital with crushed fingers. Meanwhile, her supervisor, she said, ordered her co-workers to 'start the line and look for fingers in the meat.' She returned to work that same shift. "I didn't get to rest one night," she said. "I had to work with my other hand."

She got fired about eighteen months later, on May 15, 2019. She believes it was for two reasons—one because her hand injury meant she could never return to working with the scissors needed to trim damaged parts of the birds, even though she tried until the pain became too much.

Second, she was part of a group who, on May 14, 2019, objected to Somali workers being forced to sign for safety gloves when other plant workers didn't have to follow the same procedure. The issue? If the gloves were lost, the workers would have to pay for a new pair.

Ali said other workers were fired at the same time, a day after they had protested the policy.

Among them was Hadio Wais, in her forties, who had lived in

a refugee camp for twenty years after fleeing civil wars in Somalia. She too had been injured on the job three times at Jennie-O. "The speed of the line is very fast. It's like driving a vehicle at seventy-five miles per hour," she said, as Ali translated. The first time, a machine fell from above and the machine, plus the chickens on it, knocked her over. A supervisor warned her to be more careful. "Nobody bothered if I was in pain or if I had broken anything. I was being scolded and intimidated," Wais said.

Besides issues of injuries, line speed, and bathroom breaks, Somali workers face problems in persuading employers to allow them to practice their Muslim faith at work. The U.S. Civil Rights Act of 1964 requires employers to accommodate employees' sincerely held religious beliefs unless it causes the business "undue hardship."

"Somali employees are Muslim employees, so they observe Muslim daily prayers—five times a day," Ali explained. "About two of the prayers may fall in a shift and three of them may fall outside of a work shift."

For a time at Jennie-O, Muslim prayer times were accommodated, Ali said. Supervisors or floaters would rotate through the assembly line, taking over so one or two workers at a time could leave the line, clock out, pray, and clock back in, an eight-minute process. It wasn't ideal. Precise times are prescribed for prayer, but there is leeway.

A new supervisor stopped the practice.

There are other issues—and other victories.

On April 25, 2019, Worker Memorial Day, the GMWC organized a rally at the county courthouse in St. Cloud. Because it's a day to honor workers killed or injured on the job, worker safety was at the top of a list of demands read at the courthouse. The worker center also listed the demands in a letter to Jayson Penn, chief executive of Pilgrim's Pride, a Brazilian company with U.S. headquarters in Greeley, Colorado.

Pilgrim's Pride owns the Gold'n Plump processing plant in

Cold Spring—about twenty minutes away from St. Cloud. In three inspections before Pilgrim's Pride bought the plant in 2016, OSHA had not recorded any safety violations. But that may not necessarily mean the plant is safe. GMWC published the results of a poultry worker survey noting that three in ten workers had been injured on the job. Nearly 100 percent reported being concerned about safety conditions, including fast line speed, harsh processing chemicals, wet floors, and insufficient staffing. But workers, Ali said, are reluctant to complain to management about unsafe conditions, let alone file a complaint with OSHA, for fear of being fired.

"We are asking him to make improvements in the workplace," Ali said, addressing the rally, according to an article published in the *St. Cloud Times* newspaper. "We don't have anything against the company. We want them to be in this community for the long term, but we also want to make sure that we are not creating a lot of people who have disabilities and medical conditions that they are unable to live sustainable lives." [1]

Besides safety, GMWC sought religious accommodations connected with Ramadan, the sacred month of fasting that celebrates the time that Allah, or God, gave holy scriptures, the Quran, to the Prophet Muhammad.

"Because Ramadan is sixteen hours of fasting (from sunrise to sunset), you have to eat a pre-dawn meal," Ali explained. Workers starting at 11 p.m. were being required to take their breaks earlier in their shifts. But they needed their meal breaks closer to dawn to eat enough to sustain them until sunset.

Ramadan concludes with Eid, a major holiday for Muslims celebrating the end of the fasting. "Eid is like Christmas," Ali said, noting that the plant is closed on Christmas, although Muslims would be willing to work on December 25. But some workers weren't allowed to take off on Eid. "That presented a problem," he said.

Ramadan began on May 5, 2019, ten days after the rally. For

the first time, meal breaks were changed to accommodate pre-dawn meals and Muslim workers were allowed to take an unpaid day off to celebrate Eid.

"That was a win for the workers and their families," Ali said. "We pushed hard for that."

That kind of advocacy, along with help with her on-the-job injuries, is what keeps Hadio Wais engaged, even after she was fired from the Jennie-O plant. Wais, a GMWC member, was among those who attended a demonstration at the plant on June 10, 2019.

Since GMWC opened, it has helped workers stage walkouts in order to improve conditions at several plants. In 2019, the worker center and allies successfully pushed the state legislature to pass a law making wage theft a felony.

The Greater Minnesota Worker Center "fights for workers' rights and I support them," Wais said. "It is my hope that they keep supporting us and keep supporting other workers in the future. We want to make sure they defend and support workers so they can get their rights."

12

"YOU ARE NOT ALONE"

Lucy Quintanar felt alone. She was working as a live-in nanny for a family in Houston, Texas. She was hired to take care of the children and do typical household cleaning chores. Those were the tasks that Quintanar and her employer had agreed were her job assignments. She was paid to be a nanny and housekeeper.

One day, her employer asked Quintanar to clean the swimming pool. She refused because it wasn't among the duties to which she'd agreed. The employer fired her on the spot. The family also owed her $450 for that month's work, but refused to pay her. Quintanar had been through this before with a different employer. She was not paid hundreds of dollars in wages that she'd earned.[1]

Quintanar sought help from the Fe y Justicia Worker Center. At the time, the "faith and justice" organization, with its four-person staff, was housed in a small office at St. Stephen's Episcopal Church in Houston.

Every day across the country, in homes and behind closed doors, tens of thousands of nannies, caregivers, and housekeepers report to work in entirely unregulated settings. There are no human resource departments in people's homes. There are no safety standards, no oversight, and no guarantees that they'll be afforded the protections of wage and labor laws. The circumstances are unfair on their face, but they take on an even harsher tone when considering just how foundational domestic work is to a thriving national economy. Domestic workers do the work that allows others to pursue economic mobility, security, and opportunity.

Ironically, though, domestic workers often lack access to the very legal frameworks that would give them the same opportunities to thrive and prosper in their jobs.

However, reaching and organizing domestic workers is not easy. They often work in isolation. Many are undocumented immigrants and fear the potential repercussions of visibility. Fortunately, domestic workers have learned to come together to help each other find dignity at work. They're making connections with each other and with academic partners who help them build solidarity through training.

To connect to each other, some of Fe y Justicia's members formed La Colmena (The Beehive), a group of women who met regularly to discuss their employment situations and learn about their rights. They put together a writing workshop to help each other chronicle their experiences. It led to them assembling a dozen of their stories into an anthology. *We Women, One Woman!: A View of the Lived Experience of Domestic Workers* was published and released in April 2014. The anthology features the stories of fifteen nannies, housecleaners, and caregivers who are members of La Colmena.

The anthology's stories, published in both English and Spanish, cover a range of topics, often exposing issues such as wage theft as well as unsafe and unfair working conditions. The women also described their personal lives—single motherhood, poverty, immigration, leaving their native countries and families behind—and why they felt it was so important to speak out about their workplace experiences.

Consuelo Martínez, an elder care provider, wrote in the anthology: "I'd like to express what we have to go through because for many people being a domestic worker is a job that doesn't mean anything. . . . I want everyone who hears me to remember this warrior woman who helped her children get ahead in life with an honorable job and a lot of pride."

Some of the women, including Lucy Quintanar, were less

personal in their narratives. Quintana used hers as the opportunity to call for better working conditions and collective power. "We need to get a union to get our rights, to make people conscious of the situation and the circumstances of this kind of employment. I hope everybody reads it. . . . I would like to let [other domestic workers] know that there's a place called La Colmena where they can get help to learn their rights. Don't be afraid to speak out."

Quintanar considers La Colmena part of her family. "When you're working, you don't have the opportunity to have friends," she said. "La Colmena is very important to me . . . I like belonging to a group. Now I can organize with other women to improve our labor conditions."

Laura Perez-Boston, then executive director of Fe y Justicia, knows the value of workers' voices in movements for social change.[2] "We always talk about how there's no statistic that can accurately capture what it's really like. Statistics can't tell stories."

It's easy to see how much effort and emotion was poured into the anthology, as the women who wrote its stories also handcrafted the covers of each book. One La Colmena member fashioned tiny fabric aprons that tie around the book, while another woman used Guatemalan weaving fabric to create original covers. One worker used a picture that her daughter drew of a woman with long, dark braids hugging the Earth. All of the book covers are wrapped in a scrapbooking material printed with a honeycomb design.

Mitzi Ordoñez, former domestic worker and organizer at Fe y Justicia,[3] said she and the members of La Colmena hoped the anthology would reach employers as well as other domestic workers. "We want to make employers aware of the true value of this work," she said. "Nannies and caregivers—these are jobs that make other jobs possible."

After more than eighteen years as a professional housecleaner in the suburbs of Chicago, Magdalena Zylinska said she feels very lucky. Unlike many of her fellow domestic workers, she hasn't sustained any serious injuries.

Zylinska, in her forties, cleans residences in the metropolitan Chicago area five days a week. An independent contractor, she cleans two to three houses each day. Fortunately, she doesn't do the job alone—she always works with at least one other person, so they can help each other with much of the lifting and other types of repetitive physical labor that can often lead to preventable injuries and even long-term disabilities. But Zylinska is well aware of the hazards and abuses that frequently accompany the duties of domestic workers. A workforce largely made up of immigrants and women from minority communities, domestic workers often face a level of workplace isolation that lends itself all too easily to exploitation and persistent, preventable dangers.

So when Zylinska heard an advertisement on Polish-language radio about a free training course specifically designed for domestic workers on occupational health and safety as well as green cleaning, she jumped at the chance to attend. In late 2013, she took the course and received a certificate of completion that she uses in marketing her services. During the weekend-long training course, Zylinska and her fellow domestic workers also learned about their rights under wage and labor laws and how to negotiate a contract with a client.

The course Zylinska took was developed and organized by the Arise Chicago Worker Center. The worker center is involved in campaigns to train workers on how to exercise their rights, to facilitate leadership development, and to organize collective action in communities where individuals live and work. It fills the knowledge gap recognized by Zylinska and other workers. "We don't really know what our rights are," she said. "We come from a different country, we don't know what's expected of us—a lot of [employers] will use that against us. . . . I wish more people could take this course."

Arise Chicago began reaching out to domestic workers but

found that the isolating nature of the industry made it difficult to bring workers together.

Ania Jakubek, the domestic worker organizer at Arise Chicago, said Arise started to make some real inroads after recruiting workers to participate in a national survey being conducted by the National Domestic Workers Alliance (NDWA) to develop information about conditions on the job for nannies, housekeepers, and caregivers.

The experience solidified the need for Chicago's domestic workers to organize themselves and identify personal and professional needs. Formal training and education quickly rose to the top, Jakubek said. "They wanted education related to their work. They said they didn't feel like professionals and felt like they were undervalued."

Arise organized a know-your-rights training, but Jakubek said they were not successful getting domestic workers to attend. But when they focused training on workplace safety problems faced by domestic workers, interest rose markedly. For this, Jakubek found willing partners—researchers at the University of Illinois at Chicago (UIC) School of Public Health. Together, they developed a health and safety curriculum for domestic workers that also included information on labor and wage rights.

The course offered training in green cleaning, along with a focus on three safety topics: chemical hazards, muscle and joint injuries, and work-related stress. The curriculum developers used the findings from the NDWA's survey to decide what to include in the course.

Among the survey's health and safety findings: 38 percent of respondents had suffered from work-related wrist, shoulder, elbow, or hip pain in the previous year; 29 percent of housecleaners had suffered from skin irritation; 20 percent had experienced respiratory problems; and 29 percent of caregivers had suffered a back injury in the previous twelve months.

In addition, 35 percent worked long hours without proper

breaks and 25 percent of live-in domestic workers had responsibilities that prevented them from getting at least five hours of uninterrupted sleep in the week prior to being surveyed.

Worse, the great majority of domestic workers said they didn't speak up about difficult workplace conditions for fear of losing their jobs.

The training for domestic workers at Arise Chicago is taught in Polish and Spanish. Conducted over the course of a weekend, it begins with lessons in ergonomics, such as safe lifting, bending, and carrying techniques, as well as tips on how to look for and assess hazards in the workplace. Next, the workshop covers chemical hazards and green cleaning, as many domestic workers use harsh and potentially dangerous chemicals daily to accomplish their tasks.

During this part of class, workers get some hands-on experience making their own cleaning products with more natural and less abrasive ingredients, such as vinegar, baking soda, and plain soap. Much of the green cleaning lessons were drawn from the Massachusetts organization Vida Verde, which supports Brazilian housecleaners. Marsha Love, an occupational health educator at UIC who worked with Jakubek to develop the training, said the green cleaning demonstrations are among the students' favorite lessons. In fact, one exercise has students developing an advertisement for the green cleaning products they create in class.

After ergonomics and green cleaning, discussions turn to stress—what causes stress on the job, how stress manifests, how to deal with stress collectively and as individuals, and how to address the organizational and systemic roots of stress for domestic workers. This is where education on labor rights and how to effectively negotiate with employers is especially important. To avoid stress in the employer-employee relationship, domestic workers must learn to negotiate and agree on expectations and limitations.

"The personal stress relief part is so important," Love said. "The problem for many domestic workers, especially live-ins, is that time is not their own. So to find time for stress relief is a big issue."

Jakubek said the training encourages workers to put together a stress relief "goodie bag" they can carry with them. The goodie bag could include chocolate, a soothing aromatic pouch, and pictures of their children. But, Jakubek said, it's the education on how to put together a contract and how to negotiate with clients that really gets at the root of domestic worker stress and empowers workers to celebrate and value their work. Jakubek also knows that bringing together workers who typically labor in isolated environments is a form of stress relief in itself.

Workers who complete the entire course receive a certificate. Equally important, they are encouraged to join Arise Chicago and be part of the growing domestic worker movement. "The knowledge they're getting is so important," Jakubek explained. "They're undervalued and they're not protected by most laws. We need to change that—that's one of our goals, to get them involved in policy change."

"Once workers are in the room, they feel free to speak about their needs and share their experiences and we can use that as a basis for thinking about problems and taking action on them," said Love, from UIC. "It's a very dynamic experience—the facilitator is them, not me."

Arise Chicago is not the only worker center in the Windy City reaching out to domestic workers with education and training. At the Latino Union of Chicago, organizers trained more than one hundred domestic workers in the span of four months during 2014. It was the Latino Union's first health and safety training for domestic workers. Building off their longtime partnership with UIC's Occupational and Environmental Health and Safety Education and Research Center, they brought in an industrial hygiene student to conduct focus groups with domestic workers to help identify topics for the classes.

Like the Arise Chicago courses, the Latino Union curriculum, which is delivered in English and Spanish, covers ergonomics, chemical hazards, hands-on green cleaning training, stress relief, labor rights, and employer negotiations. One feature that is unique is that it kicks off with a discussion on the history of women workers and their many accomplishments.

"We start with the idea that everyone deserves dignity and respect," explained Joe Zanoni, the now retired director of continuing education and outreach at the UIC center. "We offer some ideas, the workers offer some ideas, and hopefully we can start a conversation in which workers can support each other. We want health and safety to be a natural part of their lives."

Zanoni said organizers also offer domestic workers CPR training—a skill domestic workers had specifically requested.

Myrla Baldonado, then an organizer at Latino Union, said she had heard from many domestic workers who told her the training empowered them with the skills and confidence to initiate conversations with employers and clients. "It lifts up their spirits to see that they can change their situations," she said.[4]

The Latino Union is home to the Chicago Coalition of Household Workers. The Chicago Coalition helped advance the Illinois Domestic Workers' Bill of Rights Act, which was signed into law in 2016.

"Domestic workers have to build power," Baldonado said.

Even as their organizations were achieving success, housekeepers like Lucy Quintanar in Houston and Magdalena Zylinska in Chicago go to work each day, making beds and scrubbing bathrooms.

In the Windy City, Zylinska, who now works to organize domestic workers as a member of Arise Chicago, said she highly recommends the health and safety training to fellow workers. She also hopes the trainings will draw others into the larger movement for domestic worker rights.

No one, she said, should have to feel alone.

"Maybe we can find the solution together," Zylinska said. "Together, we have the power to change the situation."

Carly Fox, organizer, formerly with the Worker Justice Center of New York, left, with Crispin Hernandez, member, Workers' Center of Central New York, Syracuse. *I. George Bilyk*

Nora Morales, director, Centro de Derechos Laborales, Bryan, Texas. *I. George Bilyk*

Part IV

Workers and Washington

Both workers and the worker centers that represent them look to federal, state, and local governments for policies and new laws that will improve their lives—higher minimum wages, better safety standards, and access to overtime, healthcare, and paid sick leave. Sometimes those efforts are fruitful. Other times, engaging with government agencies represents a powerful threat. Terrified of deportation, many immigrant workers remain silent. When it comes to state and federal offices of occupational safety and health (OSHA)—agencies that are supposed to protect workers' safety on the job—the relationship is complicated.

> At least if OSHA regulations are passed, [employers] would have to respect these regulations and there would be fewer victims of these silent and killing illnesses. I think the work we do should not cost us our lives.
>
> —José Granados, Fe y Justicia

> I didn't get involved right away because I had fear. I thought, "I am an immigrant. I don't have rights."
>
> —José Rodriguez, a pseudonym,
> Workers' Center of Central New York

13

A FRUSTRATING FRIEND

Jonas Mendoza and José Granados sat on the stage of an auditorium in Washington, D.C. Their table was draped with royal blue fabric embossed with the emblem of the U.S. Department of Labor. At the table next to them was an administrative law judge, Daniel F. Solomon. He kept order during the proceedings in his baritone voice.

The U.S. Occupational Safety and Health Administration (OSHA) was taking public comment on a proposed regulation to protect workers who cut through bricks, granite slabs, and other silica-containing materials. Breathing in the dust can cause cancer, as well as respiratory and autoimmune disorders.

The rows of seats in the audience were filled by industry lobbyists, union representatives, a few epidemiologists, and engineers. The U.S. Chamber of Commerce and the American Chemical Council were there, as were the United Auto Workers, United Steelworkers, and North America's Building Trades Unions, all regulars at this type of proceeding.

As members of worker centers in New Jersey and Texas, Mendoza and Granados were new to Washington. But they were eager to tell their stories at the 2014 hearing. Mendoza, Granados, and other worker center members knew their experiences were different from those of union laborers. It was important for OSHA to hear from them about workplace safety.

"I dared to come here to give my testimony because I believe that most employers are not willing to do anything to prevent, remedy, or fix the problem," said José Granados from Fe y Justicia in Houston, speaking in Spanish. "At least if OSHA regulations are passed, they would have to respect these regulations and there would be fewer victims of these silent and killing illnesses. I think the work we do should not cost us our lives."

Jonas Mendoza, a member and safety liaison with New Labor in New Jersey, testified in Spanish, "There are workers who are afraid of making a complaint because of fear of losing their jobs. If the workers demand too much from their employers, they don't call you to work the next day. However, I believe that we all should have the right of safe workplaces," adding, "and that is why I am here, because I know that we can accomplish this if we combine our strengths to make the change."

Hearing from members of worker centers was a first at an OSHA rulemaking hearing. It was also the first time in its forty-plus-year history that witnesses made their presentations in Spanish. But during the Obama administration, the Labor Department was intent on reaching worker populations most at risk of workplace abuses. It meant OSHA's local offices initiating or strengthening relationships with community organizations serving immigrants, temp workers, and day laborers. The agency was motivating worker centers to provide OSHA-authorized training so members could earn an "OSHA-10" safety card. OSHA was also encouraging worker centers to apply for funding from its Susan Harwood program.

On a human level, it meant valuing the expertise of worker center leaders like Jonas Mendoza. José Granados and OSHA's assistant secretary David Michaels sent a personal letter to Mendoza to thank him for testifying at the rulemaking hearing.

"OSHA" may be a word that makes employers nervous, but in reality, it would take 134 years for the agency to inspect each workplace in the United States just once.[1] A common critique of the agency is that it is underfunded and has no teeth—fines and penalties are notoriously low, even in the most horrific cases involving death, dismemberment, and repeat egregious violations. The situation frustrates OSHA staffers as well. That's why, to make the most of its appropriation, OSHA tries to direct its attention to jobsites where workers are at greatest risk of harm or where it suspects employers are cutting corners on safety.

"When I went to OSHA in 2009, I was already familiar with community organizations around the country that were working with low-wage unorganized workers in the most dangerous jobs in the country," explained Debbie Berkowitz, who served as chief of staff at the agency until late 2015. "These organizations were mostly involved in providing assistance to workers about wage rights and preventing wage theft. They had some limited experience in dealing with worker safety issues, but didn't really have the resources to work more on safety and health."

Just before Berkowitz landed at OSHA, a worker center in Austin, Texas, issued a report about low wages and unsafe conditions for construction workers in the city—a workforce that was 78 percent Hispanic and 70 percent foreign born. A survey by the Workers Defense Project of three hundred construction workers found that two-thirds had not received safety training, and despite sweltering heat, most employers didn't allow rest breaks or provide water.

"I can't remember who I met with," Berkowitz said, "but they wanted to know why there were no OSHA fall protections in Texas. It dawned on me that during the Bush years, OSHA really disappeared. People who did not work in this field didn't have a sense of what OSHA was or that there are standards to protect people."

Keying off the worker center's report, as well as data showing that Latino construction workers were more likely to be fatally injured on the job, OSHA did an inspection blitz in Texas. Inspectors from all over the country spent a month at construction sites across the Lone Star State.

In Berkowitz's experience, the legal aid groups assisting Latino and other vulnerable or immigrant workers were not part of the wider safety and health advocacy community. "I often found that a lot of the staff were lawyers," Berkowitz explained. "They were dealing with wage theft and laws where workers can sue for lost wages, but they didn't really have experience dealing with OSHA."

There were a few worker centers, however, that had health and safety expertise. New Labor had roots with the Occupational Safety and Health Project at Rutgers University dating back to the late 1990s. The Boston Immigrant Worker Center is a project of the Massachusetts Coalition for Occupational Safety and Health.

Efforts to expand the capacity of worker centers to use health and safety for organizing were boosted in a big way by the Public Welfare Foundation based in Washington, D.C. In 2007, the foundation began awarding grants to worker centers and allied organizations engaged in labor policy, groups that spoke to the foundation's core values of racial equity, economic well-being, and fundamental fairness for all.

The Public Welfare Foundation's Workers' Rights program was directed by Bob Shull. He viewed wage theft and unsafe workplaces as affronts to "the most fundamental expectations of work: that you will put some money in your pocket and come home alive, well, and in one piece so that you and your family can benefit from your position as an employee."[2] Shull was one of the few in the foundation world who recognized occupational health and safety as a justice and equity issue, not just a topic for technicians and engineers. He recognized the potential for deepening the expertise of worker centers to expand their membership and, with that, their influence.

From 2007 through 2011, the Public Welfare Foundation awarded $8.7 million to worker centers and partner organizations. Its investment in community labor organizations continued through 2020 and totaled more than $25 million.

OSHA also has its own grant-making program. The Susan

Harwood Training Grant Program awards about $10 million each year to help organizations provide health and safety education and training to workers and small businesses. "It has always been geared to organizations that have done some outreach and education on worker safety and could reach a target population of workers exposed to serious hazards," Berkowitz said. The grant applications came largely from nonprofit business groups, unions, and universities, but not community labor organizations like worker centers.

"We thought it was important to let groups that connect with these vulnerable workers in high-risk jobs know there was a program at OSHA called the Harwood grants that could enable them to hire a specialist to do health and safety training. With the funding, they could expand their work beyond wage and hour violations. There's another set of issues—job safety and health— and the groups could build their capacity and have a big impact," Berkowitz explained.

Shull helped organize an all-day workshop to introduce his grantees to OSHA's Susan Harwood program. He pulled in some of his counterparts from other foundations who were funding immigrant rights' groups. Berkowitz assigned OSHA speakers to explain the technical details of applying for federal grants, an intimidating pursuit for nonprofits with razor-thin staff. She also arranged for speakers who were current Harwood grantees to offer lessons from their own experiences.

The National Council for Occupational Safety and Health (National COSH) was a regular recipient of the Harwood grants. Its executive director, Tom O'Connor, was one speaker and later continued as a mentor to the worker centers. "He helped a lot of people because he knew how to do education for low-wage workers on OSHA and worker rights," Berkowitz explained. "We had all these groups that were important to fund who had never done education on worker safety before."

For several years, O'Connor led an annual gathering of the

worker centers and National COSH grantees. "They would share information on the best techniques to teach workers complicated health and safety information so that the new grantees would succeed doing this work and doing it in a way that it would be impactful and effective," Berkowitz added.

From 2010 through 2017, the OSHA Harwood program granted about $1 million each year to worker centers. Some were awarded to individual centers, such as the Workers Defense Project, Brazilian Worker Center in Massachusetts, and Make the Road New York. Umbrella organizations, such as Interfaith Worker Justice and the National Day Labor Organizing Network, also received grants, which they distributed to worker centers in their networks.

The grants were useful, said Adam Kader, director of the Arise Chicago Worker Center. "They helped us figure out how we incorporate a health and safety rights framework within our practice," he said. "We've been doing workshops forever. The change with the Harwood is that it allowed us to incorporate more pieces of health and safety. In our intakes, we'd start to probe for things, precisely because workers wouldn't voluntarily say them. That's the benefit of it.

"It was about expertise and honestly, me personally, we didn't know that much about health and safety. We know a lot more now," Kader added.

In 2011, the Worker Justice Center of New York (WJCNY) received its first OSHA grant. Its staff and collaborators would provide safety training in Spanish to farmworkers and dairy hands in seven counties in central New York.

"It was a huge important source of funding," said Carly Fox, a former worker advocate with WJCNY. "We were seeing a health and safety crisis. People couldn't believe how many people had died in dairy in New York State. The OSHA trainings were good because they got us to the farms and we were talking to workers," Fox said. "But with those grants there was a lot of pressure to produce numbers. You can't build relationships through that funding."

By the third year of Harwood funding, WJCNY and the Workers' Center of Central New York decided to capitalize on being permitted on the farms. They would interview workers as part of a larger research project to document labor conditions in the state's dairy industry. As they collected workers' stories about the prevalence of dangerous conditions and the resulting injuries, the data became a call to action. Workers mobilized to push OSHA to focus attention on the dairy industry. They persisted. They succeeded, as OSHA began inspecting local farms.

Ultimately, a worker center's goal is "about the workers having power and us facilitating that the workers have power," Fox noted. "Not just one-off trainings."

Worker centers also have their eyes wide open when it comes to the OSHA Harwood grants. The training topics are prescribed and the written materials are pre-approved. Some subject matter is off-limits, such as workers' compensation, because it does not fall under OSHA jurisdiction. For worker centers, the approach requires segregating OSHA-funded content from exercises that probe worker-employer dynamics. "It's not just training that matters," explained Lou Kimmel, New Labor's executive director. "If the boss tells you to do something, you might still do it. It's how to evaluate: 'Is my life at risk? How do we approach the boss about it? How do we talk to workers? How do we make the hard decisions to reject the work?'"

Since 2014, New Labor has received about $150,000 per year in OSHA Harwood grants. But Kimmel noted, "If we're just a training center, we're not building power."

Understanding their safety rights gives workers options. Even the threat of filing an OSHA complaint can pressure employers, said Shelly Ruzicka, communications director at Arise Chicago. "Sometimes anything from the government is real scary." Workers will ask for a meeting with management and say, "Well, if you're refusing to even meet, then we're going to file these complaints with OSHA," Ruzicka said, with workers pointing out that they'd rather "settle it and negotiate directly because that's faster."

There's benefit for OSHA, too. With only 1,815 inspectors nationwide for nearly 144 million workers, they want to reach workers most at risk.

Worker centers help them do that.

14

"THEY KIND OF HAVE
US LIKE THE COWS"

An autumn snow covered the farmyards, leaving odds and ends
of dried stalks poking through the blanketed fields. Everything seemed bleak and cheerless, even the three large tabby cats
who skulked outside the tired beige ranch house, windows cur-
tained with cardboard and sheets.

Farmworker organizer Carly Fox pulled her car into the driveway and hopped out of the driver's seat. Crispin Hernandez,
another organizer, followed close behind, past the cats, to knock
on the doors and windows.

Sometimes fighting for workers' rights means courtroom battles and lawyers' briefs.

That's how it had been for Hernandez, who was the plaintiff in
a landmark suit challenging a New York State law that excludes
farmworkers from the state's employee relations act. He has also
been part of a group pushing legislators in Albany to change
the law.

In his suit, Hernandez asserted that the 1937 State Employment Relations Act, which excludes farmworkers from the right to
organize, runs counter to the New York State Constitution, which
protects all employees' right to collectively bargain. At stake was
the right of the state's sixty thousand farmworkers, many of them
immigrants, to negotiate wages and working conditions.

But, on that cold November morning in rural upstate New
York, fighting for workers' rights meant driving on back roads,

looking for the kind of lonely, rundown homes or trailers that telegraph the situation of those living inside—dairy workers, mostly immigrants, trying to catch some sleep between either brutally long, or brutally short, shifts taken up with milking hundreds of cows.

"The farmers say that the workers' lives are good, that they live good, but the majority of the farms are really bad," Hernandez said. He worked on dairy farms for years until he became a staff member at the Workers' Center of Central New York (WCCNY). WCCNY's office is in Syracuse. At the time, Fox was working for the Worker Justice Center of New York in Rochester. She has since left her position and is working with other worker groups in upstate New York.

"People come here with debt, plus they need to send money home to the family," Hernandez said, speaking through an interpreter. "We're working in this kind of job because we don't have legal status—bad housing, exploitation by the farmers, threats from the bosses, and the challenges of not being able to speak English. They kind of have us like the cows."

Organizing dairy workers isn't easy. First, they are remote, working in rural areas far from one another and far from any towns. They live isolated on farms, only occasionally leaving to buy food. Most say they don't speak English well, and only half have completed between nine and twelve years of formal education, according to the 2016 survey of Hispanic dairy workers in New York State conducted by Cornell University.[1]

Even with those challenges, there's an advantage to organizing dairy farmworkers, beyond dairy being the largest agricultural industry in the state. Unlike most farmworkers, who follow the harvest, never living long enough in any one place to forge lasting connections to advocacy groups, dairy farmworkers milk cows year-round. So, despite high turnover, dairy workers tend to remain at the same farm for longer periods.

•   •   •

Farmwork is the most dangerous industry in the nation, with more than 6,300 agricultural workers dying from work-related injuries from 2008 through 2018, according to the U.S. Bureau of Labor Statistics.[2] That fatality rate is nearly seven times higher than the rate for all other workers. At the same time the worker centers were preparing their New York dairy campaign, the state's health department identified thirty-four deaths on dairy farms between 2007 and 2012.[3]

Hosting free health and safety training sessions funded by the U.S. Occupational Safety and Health Administration (OSHA) enabled advocates to connect with more dairy workers. Fox and Rebecca Fuentes, then the lead organizer at WCCNY, offered trainings at churches and homes—safe spaces for workers who feared attracting the attention of their employers.[4]

Over time, Fox and Fuentes, through their respective centers, added three other effective strategies to augment legislative and legal pursuits: they persuaded OSHA to initiate a Local Emphasis Program, which would include unannounced inspections of dairy farms; they authored a groundbreaking report on dairy farm conditions; and they set up a sanctuary home in downtown Syracuse.

Those strategies laid the groundwork for two important legislative victories, both won in the summer of 2019. In July, New York governor Andrew Cuomo signed the Farm Laborers Fair Labor Practices Act, correcting a 1937 state law that prevented farmworkers from forming unions. A month earlier, Cuomo had signed a bill to authorize driver's licenses for all, including undocumented farmworkers.

In addition, working up the food chain from cow to consumer product, the workers had held several meetings with representatives from Chobani, urging the yogurt company, a major buyer of milk products, to back dairy farmworkers' rights to form a union.

Meanwhile, in rural New York, driving from dairy farm to dairy farm, the miles add up, quickly.

On that snowy day in November 2018, when Hernandez and

Fox knocked on the door of the beige house, someone finally peered through a curtain, then cautiously opened the door, eyes bloodshot. Hernandez and Fox went inside and delivered some leaflets before leaving. They had awakened him. He told them he had worked so many twelve-hour overnight shifts milking cows that he hadn't seen the sun in days.

It's not an unfamiliar story to worker leader José Rodriguez, who recounted life on a dairy farm during a long drive in lightly falling snow to a fundraising dance on the other side of the state. The dance was sponsored by the Alianza Agricola, a farmworker-led grassroots organization.

"My father was a coffee farmer," Rodriguez said, speaking through an interpreter. His name has been changed to protect his privacy. "We had four or five cows. We milked them by hand and sold the milk. We worked in the dairy farm culture."

Rodriguez had an ambition to add a few more hectares to the family farm, buy a pickup truck, and diversify the crops grown there, moving between lemon trees and coffee bushes. But in Mexico, opportunities for someone like him to build enough wealth are almost nonexistent, he said.

And so Rodriguez, like many others, crossed the border to the United States, making his way to the dairy farms in New York where an older brother worked. But nothing about his upbringing milking cows on his family farm in Mexico prepared Rodriguez for the scale of the farms and the strain of the work caring for cows in upstate New York, where dairy farming is a major industry, worth $14 billion to the state economy.[5]

When Rodriguez first arrived from Mexico, he worked on a nine-thousand-cow farm in the maternity department where cows, about to calve, required constant monitoring. The cows are agitated and become even more so when their newborn calves are taken away. "The cows get *brava*, aggressive," he said. "You have to be alert. It's dangerous."

Rodriguez, who stayed in farm-funded housing, said he earned between $7 and $8 an hour and slept three to a room on an inflatable mattress. "We had to step over the others" to get to work.

Rodriguez would milk cows from 5 a.m. to 9:30 a.m. After a break, he might move wood chips, change the cows' bedding, move the cows, and clean the milk machines. Shifts lasted twelve hours. If Rodriguez had worked on one of the smaller farms, he might have been assigned to rotate on and off duty every four hours, making it impossible to get a full eight hours' rest between milkings.

"The cows can also injure workers. They kick," Rodriguez said. "They kicked one worker and he lost his teeth. Sometimes they kick you in the arms and the chest. When you are moving the cows to get milk, some of them are in heat and they push on you."

"The bulls that impregnate the cows are aggressive by nature," Rodriguez said. He saw one worker get kicked by a bull and then saw the man's brother carrying him. "I know they did several operations on him."

"In cold weather, it's very slippery. It's a wet environment and it gets icy," he said. Falls are a constant hazard. "One day, I was running after a cow that had run away and I fell on my back. My whole body was sore."

Mountains of silage and corn must be maintained by removing a top layer that tends to spoil. "In times of snow, you have to clean it, but it is very slippery. You have to be very careful. You don't want to hurry," Rodriguez said. Yet "there's never an employer who will tell you, 'Don't hurry. Don't exploit yourselves. If you are not careful, you will fall.'"

The manure lagoon is dangerous. "I had a brother fall in. I don't know how he got out. You can die of inhalation or just drown." Compounding the dangers, "the pressure to produce is enormous. There's always so much to do and not enough time. You feel you have to produce, or you'll be fired," Rodriguez said.

"One danger is the pressure and the other is how many hours you have to work and how much rest you get. The pressure. You are leaving your family, your wife sometimes, your kids. You have a lot of personal worries," he said. "You don't know what's in your head. It's like being in two worlds. You are here, but you feel like you are in two worlds."

Rodriguez himself was injured—one time in a fall that left him unable to work for days, another time with a finger so badly cut that it needed stitches and time to heal so it wouldn't get infected. Yet the farmer demanded that he work. At one farm, bedbugs had overrun the mattresses. At another farm, he and five other workers came down with an illness with high fevers, so high that they were given antibiotics. They were still told to report for work.

Like Crispin Hernandez, Rodriguez became acquainted with Fox and Fuentes. "I was interested," he said, "but I didn't get involved right away because I had fear. I thought, 'I am an immigrant. I don't have rights.'"

Rodriguez didn't know, for example, that New York farmworkers injured on the job have a right to apply for workers' compensation. The insurance would cover the medical costs for a work-related injury. It would also pay part of his wages if he had to miss work for more than seven days on a doctor's order. He also didn't understand why, if he got hurt, the farmer would insist that he tell medical personnel that he had been injured during off hours. The farmer didn't want his insurance premiums to increase.

Since Rodriguez joined Fuentes at the WCCNY, he has organized a meeting at the onion farm where he worked after he left his last dairy job and attended countless protests and rallies. "Besides learning about my rights, I have become educated about outreach, unions, and minimum wages," Rodriguez said. "I'm feeling more confidence now and freedom, because I know my rights."

Both Rodriguez and Hernandez's involvement with the WCCNY started around 2013, which is about when Fox and Fuentes met them. But on opposite ends of the state, the two women, separately, had already begun working in the dairy industry a year earlier.

Fox had been assigned to visit dairies as part of her job as a paralegal with the Worker Justice Center of New York (WJCNY).

Fuentes's mother, a Mexican, had been an immigrant farmworker in California, where Fuentes was born. As a teenager, Fuentes was a domestic worker. Her employers gave her a closet to sleep in. "I knew that if I didn't have documents, I would have had to live under those conditions," she said. Instead she quit and joined the U.S. Army, assigned to Fort Drum in upstate New York, where she later graduated from college. "I couldn't find much of a Latino community here, but I wanted to help."

In 2005, an explosion at an Oswego County farm killed one undocumented worker and injured nine others, capturing local headlines. "The explosion required so many people to get involved," Fuentes said. "That accident brought together not only advocates for workers' rights, but also advocates for immigrants. It was one layer after another."

Her involvement deepened as she volunteered to sit with undocumented workers in court. "I began to feel useful," she said.

"I started to understand more about organizing," Fuentes said. "I learned to speak in front of people. People are afraid too, but there's nothing like speaking up because your story is powerful."

Fuentes and Fox's outreach to farmworkers was, in part, funded through OSHA's Susan Harwood Training Grants Program. Even so, the relationship between farmworkers and OSHA is complicated. Some farms, depending on size, aren't covered by OSHA. Some are. The details are confusing. But either way, workers are entitled to know about their rights concerning job hazards.

With their OSHA grants, Fox and Fuentes also taught farmworkers how to file OSHA complaints. "People were afraid to file, they were afraid of being identified," Fuentes said.

"The OSHA trainings were good because they got us to the farms and we were talking to workers," Fox said. "But with those grants there was a lot of pressure to produce numbers. You can't build relationships through that funding."

One night, during a phone call that lasted for hours, Fox and Fuentes talked out their frustrations in what turned out to be a pivotal conversation. Fox remembers finally lying on the floor in her office, propping the phone up against her shoulder, so she and Fuentes could keep wrestling with the piecemeal nature of their efforts. A training here, a training there, but no real change.

If any change was going to happen, they concluded before hanging up, exhausted, the workers had to be the ones leading it. Their focus shifted and, in 2013, as it did, they met Rodriguez and Hernandez, along with many others.

Knowing the power of stories, they began to gather them in a very deliberate way through a grant landed by Gretchen Purser, chair of the WCCNY's board and an associate professor of sociology at Syracuse University. The grant funded a study of working conditions on dairy farms.

"Basically, we used that study as a way of doing outreach and meeting more farmworkers, because we had to travel all over the state to implement this survey," Purser said. "So that became a way of building a base of farmworker members for the organization."

The study involved a two-hundred-plus-question survey and many hour-long interviews, conducted one worker at a time. Just the act of listening was powerful. "Eighty-eight people got their story told," and they told others about being heard, Fox said.

Besides relationships, the organizers were building knowledge.

"We started doing research about the problems," Fuentes said. "The farmers were using chloroform to prevent fungus in the cows' feet. One worker was mixing it with no gloves. It splashed in his eye. He was blind for thirty minutes and nobody was around to help him. He was in such pain and used the water for the cows to drink to splash his eyes."

That was the worker's third significant work-related injury. Earlier, a cow had pushed him, and he had a serious fall. He told

Fuentes, "'I'm quitting. My life is worth more than $7.25 an hour,'" she said. "He left, but he left us his story, he left us a video, and he helped us connect," Fuentes said. He also filed an OSHA complaint, co-signing it with another worker.

Researching, Fuentes also learned about and decided to pursue OSHA's Local Emphasis Program, which allows OSHA area offices to focus on high-hazard industries. Facing intense opposition from the state's dairy coalition, the worker groups countered with an eleven-day, twenty-three-stop lobbying and media blitz. The effort paid off as OSHA instituted its industry focus to more closely monitor New York's dairy farms.

The media blitz, of course, attracted attention; it was the most public part of the two-year struggle to increase OSHA's involvement. With that, conditions began to improve as farmers, worried about what the government agency might do, upgraded their operations.

"The workers got to see that change," Fuentes said.

Meanwhile, organizing continued. Crispin Hernandez, the worker named on the New York dairy lawsuit, became more active. Hernandez came to the United States in 2012, but before he left Mexico, he had an unnerving experience. The body of a Mexican farmworker who was killed while working on a dairy farm in New York State was returned to the man's family, not far from Hernandez's hometown. Hernandez didn't know the man, but the news spread. Even so, by that time, at age seventeen, Hernandez had made up his mind to come to the United States and work on New York's dairy farms.

Only a few months after he arrived, a cow stepped on his hand. His fingers were crushed, but the owner wouldn't take him to the hospital, Hernandez said. Bugs infested the crowded housing where he and the other workers lived. Chemicals soaked through the gloves and boots given to them by the farm owners; if they wanted better ones, they had to buy them with their own money.

In 2014, disillusioned, Hernandez began attending WCCNY meetings whenever he could make the ninety-mile trip to Syracuse on one of his days off from Marks Farm in rural Lowville. But on March 24, 2015, something happened that would accelerate his commitment.

Hernandez ended up waiting with one of his fellow workers, named Francisco, while arrangements were made to get him to the emergency room. Farmworker advocates say that a Marks Farm manager, the husband of one of the owners, had not only fired Francisco, but assaulted him, kicking him and throwing him to the ground, where he hit his head on a metal part of a wheel. With the help of WCCNY, Francisco filed complaints with OSHA and the local police.

The farm insisted the worker was at fault.

Six weeks later, on International Workers' Day, May 1, 2015, the worker centers, along with farmworkers, staged a protest outside of Marks Farms. The rally attracted dozens, with participants calling for an end to abusive workplace conditions.

"At this time, we are kind of under the radar doing this work of organizing workers, putting in OSHA complaints and developing leadership," Fuentes said. "We organized that rally and we had a lot of media. We had a lot of public awareness about it. I think that put a lot of pressure on the police and everybody to, at least, do something."

None of the Marks Farm employees attended the rally, but "Crispin was really important in organizing it" and he watched it from the window of his trailer, Fuentes said, talking about Hernandez. "He made calls to allies. He did some interviews. Crispin had seen that worker get beat up and that motivated him to be more involved."

After the protest, Hernandez began to organize a workers committee on Marks Farm. His employers noticed. Soon, Hernandez was switched to a less desirable job. "Crispin came to the realization that he had to do something openly, not just in hiding. They had already retaliated against him. We talked about that. What is the next step? We were doing all this work under the radar. Sometimes there is more protection when you are out in the open," Fuentes said.

On August 24, 2015, a few months after the rally, Hernandez and his fellow workers invited Fuentes to the farm to discuss health and safety risks, the lack of personal protective equipment, and forming a workers committee. The farmers called the police, who came, but made no arrests. For Fuentes and the workers, it was terrifying.

Often, in organizing, advocates try to protect themselves and workers, particularly those who are undocumented, Fuentes said. "But you have to have these moments where you have to push and agitate. Our job is together to take a step forward, confront fear, get to the other side, celebrate, and keep going. Otherwise we're not going to make progress."

The police encounter had its effect, however, Fuentes said. Support for the fledgling worker movement at Marks Farm dwindled to two—Hernandez and one other farmhand. The week after the meeting, the two went from worker house to worker house handing out flyers about workers' rights. They were both fired soon after, on September 1, 2015.

"It was retaliation," Fox said. "It was the perfect case of worker retaliation for organizing." According to Fuentes, the farm claimed the dismissal was due to the falling price of milk.

While all that was going on, the WCCNY solidified the third part of its strategy—this one outlined in wood and siding, not politics or lawsuits. The center was given the use of a house, a rambling two-story home in a run-down neighborhood in Syracuse. They called it La Casa.

"That was the importance of La Casa—so people could come and stay there if they lost their jobs," Fuentes said. When Hernandez was fired, he lost his housing on the farm and had one week to find a new place to live. At one point, La Casa, once owned by a former priest, housed Hernandez, Rodriguez, and the family of a farmworker victimized by domestic violence.

"It is pretty terrifying to think about, you know, speaking up, losing your job, literally having to be out on the streets, as an undocumented worker," Purser said.

With so much to lose and so many grave consequences, it's not a surprise that many would be too afraid to organize to better their conditions. "We always wanted to have a place that we could offer workers as a way to organize them and overcome their fear," Fuentes said. "A sanctuary."

Meanwhile, lawyers from the New York Civil Liberties Union (NYCLU) were looking hard at the experience Hernandez had at the Marks Farm when he and a co-worker were fired shortly after distributing the pamphlets.

Eight months after Hernandez lost his job, on May 10, 2016, the NYCLU filed *Hernandez v. New York* in the state's Supreme Court. The suit aimed to overturn the 1937 State Employment Relations Act, which prohibited farmworkers from unionizing, even though the state's bill of rights guaranteed a right of representation. Aadhithi Padmanabhan, the NYCLU lawyer who took on Hernandez's case, said the 1937 act discriminates against farmworkers. "They are a historically disenfranchised group of people and it violates their right to equal protection."

Just hours after the NYCLU filed Hernandez's lawsuit, New York governor Andrew Cuomo announced that his administration would not fight the suit: "This clear and undeniable injustice must be corrected." Cuomo's statement validated the farmworkers' complaints. The possibility of a court ruling in favor of Hernandez and the worker centers now seemed less remote.

"It would mean that New York is recognizing these workers who've been invisible for so long," said Padmanabhan. "People like Crispin are so brave to put themselves on the line like this—it's a huge leap for workers like him to take this kind of risk and fight for their rights."[6]

For Fuentes, it was already something to celebrate. "It's a huge victory for workers like Crispin," Fuentes said of the worker-led lawsuit. "It's been a lot of work for him—just imagine the pressure with his name on a lawsuit like this."

Although the State of New York declined to contest the lawsuit, another party was ready for the fight. The New York Farm Bureau was allowed to intervene in the case. The bureau is the state's largest agricultural trade and lobbying group. "Any kind of confining work agreements can be difficult for farms to deal with when uncertainty is so much a part of agriculture," Farm Bureau communications director Steve Ammerman told a reporter from Documented, a news organization covering immigration in New York.[7]

Fox and Fuentes knew that Hernandez's case was just one fight in an uphill battle toward safer and fairer workplaces, perhaps even a union. Win or lose, "the bigger point here is building worker power—they are at the front and center of these actions," said Fox.

The best way to protect the rights of workers is to tell them about their rights. "Then you can add other things that are not protected," Fuentes said. "We weren't talking about unions back then. We were just talking about a group of people getting together on their own time in their own houses, and that's freedom of association."

Fox agreed. "Whether there's a union or not, workers are going to organize. If we gain these protections, it'll be another tool that we can use. But what's really important is holding government accountable, pushing for new laws, pushing for new strategies. This lawsuit isn't the end."

On June 27, 2017, as Hernandez's case was making its way through the court system, the WJCNY and the WCCNY released *Milked: Immigrant Dairy Farmworkers in New York State*. *Milked* was based on a survey of farmworkers as well as interviews Fox, Fuentes, and others had conducted across the state. The timing was deliberate, with the release pegged for National Dairy Month, an eighty-plus-year tradition kicked off by the New York state legislature with "Dairy Day."

The dairy industry contributes $14 billion annually to New York's economy.[8] Milk is the state's top agricultural commodity, with the state ranking number one nationwide in the production of cottage cheese, sour cream, and yogurt.[9] On the surface, the situation seems like a bright spot in upstate New York's struggling economy. But underneath the idyllic stereotype of the family farm, workers had been increasingly coming forward to report hazardous working conditions, wage violations, and employer abuse.

The dairy boom over the last decade meant higher production—up 22 percent between 2007 and 2018, from 986 million pounds of milk to 1.3 billion pounds. But it has been happening at fewer farms, 4,295 farms in 2018, down almost 1,400 farms from 5,683 in 2007.[10] More farms are factory-like, many with herds of one thousand cows or more. They often rely on immigrant guest workers and unauthorized labor.

"When we released the report, we got a ton of media attention," recalled Purser. "That was an opportunity for the workers themselves to talk to the public, so they did a speaking tour all over the state. They talked to the media a bunch of times. So basically, the leadership of these workers was developing more and more."

Milked is based on interviews with eighty-eight dairy workers from fifty-three different farms. The project was a collaboration of WCCNY, WJCNY, and researchers with Cornell and Syracuse Universities, including Purser, who co-wrote the report.

Most of the workers interviewed worked in large operations with five hundred or more cows and shared their tasks with fewer than eleven nonfamily employees. Nearly all were born in Mexico or Guatemala—93 percent were unauthorized and 73 percent spoke little or no English. Hourly wages averaged $9 over a twelve-hour shift. Workers said they left their farms about every eleven days and felt "locked-up" because of the long work hours, inability to get a driver's license, and fear of immigration enforcement. Nearly three-quarters indicated that their principal safety concern was aggressive cows and bulls. They complained of substandard housing with insect infestations, holes in walls and floors, and inadequate ventilation.

To draw more media attention, the workers decided to release *Milked* at a rally in New York City, where workers were hosted by members of the Service Employees International Union. The place chosen? Chobani SoHo, a yogurt bar in one of Manhattan's chic neighborhoods.

"We were learning more about the food chain and the milk industry," Fuentes said. "We learned that those who make the most profit are the ones at the top, like Chobani." They noted that Hamdi Ulukaya, a Turkish immigrant, owns Chobani. "We wanted him to know about the immigrants on his food chain." Chobani has the highest share of the U.S. yogurt market.

"It's such a successful industry right now and production is increasing so fast, but we're not giving credit as to why," Fox said. "These workers work incredible hours. They're afraid of getting fired and their immigration status is used to keep them in fear. It's a very troubled industry. This isn't dignified work. It's substandard."

The dairy workers delivered *Milked* to the store manager at the Chobani SoHo. Soon upper management reached out, asking for a meeting. Several meetings ensued. The company announced that it would partner with Fair Trade USA, a third-party certification organization, to develop standards for dairy farms. Fuentes said Chobani officials were surprised when the workers weren't satisfied.

"This is precisely the problem," Fuentes said. "Things are supposed to be for the workers, but they don't have a voice in it. Chobani is just creating something on its own and implementing it without us. We represent two hundred workers in this industry. Chobani should be talking to us, to the workers themselves."

In a November 2019 letter to Chobani, the WCCNY and others reminded Chobani that in 2018, twenty-four labor groups and others wrote to the Fair Trade USA in alarm. They told the association that one of its certified farms was firing, harassing, and intimidating workers who were trying to form a union. Fuentes said the dairy workers are waiting to see how Chobani's certification program plays out.

But Chobani didn't agree to the dairy workers' demands— Chobani's support, or at least its neutrality, if dairy farmworkers want to unionize.

For Hernandez, the work has been exhausting. Fuentes and Fox have tried to protect him from the constant pressure of being the face of a struggle that is far larger than one man in his mid-twenties, who was just seventeen when he left his home in Mexico. "It affects me a lot," Hernandez said, as he drove from farm to farm on that snowy November day. "I feel like the work I've been doing has impacted my mental health. I don't feel safe. I sometimes feel like I can't keep going.

"I feel like I'm a target. I know people don't like that I'm talking about the situation of workers," he said. "But the reason I'm motivated is that the people support me.

"I'm doing this because it is so important and we know what is happening throughout all New York State," Hernandez said. "Our lives are really important, and they need to treat us with dignity and respect."

Epilogue

Six months after the *Milked* report's June 2017 release, a lower court granted the New York Farm Bureau's motion to dismiss *Hernandez v. New York*. It was a major blow.

The New York Civil Liberties Union appealed, winning its

case.[11] On May 23, 2019, in a 4–1 decision, the court declared the State Employment Relations Act unconstitutional. The decision paved the way for farmworkers to collectively bargain. The New York Farm Bureau quickly announced its plan to appeal the decision.[12]

Shortly after that, however, the bureau decided not to appeal because momentum was building in Albany to amend the State Employment Relations Act to include farmworkers. Signed by Governor Andrew Cuomo on July 17, 2019, the amendments, known as the Farm Laborers Fair Labor Practices Act, guaranteed overtime, a rest day, the right to unionize, and health and safety protections. Some organizations representing agricultural businesses objected to other aspects of the act, but the parts improving conditions for the farmworkers went into effect on January 1, 2020.

15

DIAPER POWER

Time and time again, Alma Garcia, Nancy Plankey-Videla, and Nora Morales crowded into Garcia's mobile home to chop lettuce, slice tomatoes, and prepare special red tortillas, loading Styrofoam boxes with Garcia's *enchiladas potosinas, flautas,* and *gorditas,* cooked in the style she learned as a young girl growing up in the state of San Luis Potosí in Mexico.

Rent was due for use of the back room of a beauty parlor housed in a worn gas-station strip mall on a flat stretch of nondescript highway in rural Texas.

With enough enchiladas—and they were popular—the leaders of the Centro de Derechos Laborales (CDL) could come up with the $300 to keep the office open in the beauty parlor and continue the fight for workers' rights.

For CDL, it was a fight that began in a textbook way and progressed to a couple of dozen adults wearing diapers outside a Texas poultry plant. In October 2018, they were there to protest working conditions at Sanderson Farms, Inc., one of the largest employers in Brazos County, home of the Aggies at Texas A&M University.

"I believe that was one of our greatest achievements because this city is very small, very conservative, and I don't think they had seen something like that," said Morales, one of Garcia's sous chefs on enchilada duty and also, with Garcia, one of CDL's two part-time staffers at the time.

"Outside of the plant? Never!" said Garcia, speaking through a translator and using a pseudonym to protect her privacy.

In 2014, when CDL began, no one was thinking about diapers.

"We wanted to work from the bottom, from the base up," said Morales, speaking through a translator during a December 2018 interview. Morales, now the center's director, had come to CDL's founding organization, the Brazos Interfaith Immigration Network, for help with a wage theft problem at another company. Through the network's intervention, Morales got back about half of what she was owed.

At first CDL was organizing itself using an approach advocated by Saul Alinsky. The acclaimed writer, now deceased, is considered to be the father of community organizing. The women described Alinsky's approach as more of a top-down model.

But that shifted when they met Martha Ojeda, the senior national organizer for Interfaith Worker Justice (IWJ). At the time, she was executive director of Fe y Justicia, a worker center in Houston, just a hundred miles down Texas State Highway 6. Ojeda's involvement had a significant impact on Bryan's fledgling group. Through her, they made connections with other worker centers around the country striving to improve conditions for poultry workers. They felt less isolated in their work.

Ojeda taught them another very important lesson—the importance of organizing from the bottom up.

At first, Morales said, "We were doing what we thought was needed. We thought we knew their problem and we wanted to help them solve it. We didn't realize that, perhaps, they had a different problem they really wanted us to help them resolve."

Early on, for example, CDL decided to focus on workers not being paid when they were changing in and out of the aprons, coats, hair nets, gloves, and other gear to prevent contamination of the chicken and to stave off the damp and cold inside the plant, Morales said. "But they weren't worried about that. They were worried about permission to go to the bathroom, about the chemicals [used to disinfect the raw chicken], about sexual harassment, about the misuse of the FMLA [Family Medical Leave Act], and injuries to their wrists."

Through Fe y Justicia, CDL connected with National COSH (the National Council for Occupational Safety and Health), a broad network of labor advocates, educators, and health professionals concerned about worker safety. Those connections linked them to the Poultry Worker Justice Campaign funded by Oxfam America, an international charitable organization aiming to alleviate poverty worldwide.

"First of all, we learned that what happens here is happening at all the poultry plants," Morales said. It was helpful "to see how other centers were working, to see what we could implement here, and begin to work together."

Some of the tips were practical—more pictures, fewer words in training materials. "Not all workers have the same level of education, so that's what we had to take note of," Morales said.

By 2017, CDL had coalesced, recruiting through brochures, open houses, Facebook pages, and word-of-mouth by individuals who had been helped by the worker center. Leaders gathered testimonies from workers employed at Sanderson Farms, collecting photographs of skin damaged by chemicals and of wrists, hands, and arms swollen by the fast line speed and repetitive motion of cutting thousands of chickens per shift.

"We had the support of the IWJ and Martha Ojeda, who helped to train us, so we could identify the different points, the different ways that workers' rights were being violated," Garcia said. The workers, for example, meeting in the back room of the beauty parlor, drew diagrams of the assembly line at the plant, identifying the pressure points where injuries occurred.

"One of the main problems is that they weren't given permission to go to the bathroom. And so, women who were pregnant—their conditions were precarious," Garcia said. "Since there were people who weren't given permission to go to the bathroom, they would wear adult diapers.

"The break isn't enough time to go to the restroom because there are so many people who work there and there aren't enough bathrooms, and the bathrooms that are there, about half of them are broken," she said. "There was one worker who peed on himself when he wasn't allowed to go to the bathroom. They wouldn't give him permission to go and change, either, so he left the job."

They learned about other issues, mostly related to the ever-increasing speed of the production line. Chickens come through the line sitting on cones so workers can trim wings and thighs. "But the knives and the scissors are dull, so they have to work harder and it's more dangerous," Garcia said.

In another section, the dead chickens on conveyor belts need to be hung on overhead hooks for eviscerating. "Right now, they are talking about forty-five birds a minute," maybe double that using two hands, Morales said. And because the birds are packed so tightly on the conveyor belts, the workers have to yank on them before hanging them. "That's why we have so many workers who have injuries to their shoulders and their hands."

Chemicals used to disinfect the carcasses pose another problem. Workers' "eyes tear up. Their noses run. They are breathing it. They say they feel like they have bronchitis, but it's really the chemicals," Garcia said. "There was one worker—the chemicals splashed in her eyes and she's seriously affected. She's losing her eyesight and still has recurring problems. Also, her arms and her wrists are injured. She's a young woman with four children."

The workers, they learned, were given protective gear—an apron and gloves—but too often they tore because they were made of flimsy plastic. When the gear ripped, the company wouldn't replace it. Instead, workers had to buy replacement gear with their own money from a vending machine that also stocked protective eyeglasses and ear plugs. They didn't know what chemicals were being used, even though the U.S. Occupational Safety and

Health Administration (OSHA) regulations require workers to be informed.

"If your head hurts a lot and you go to the infirmary," Garcia said, "they don't have anything for a headache. But interesting, *they* don't have any medicine. But the vending machine is full of medicine."

Sexual harassment was also an issue, with supervisors trying to date workers. "It's like quid pro quo harassment. 'You do what I say, and then I'll give you something,'" Garcia said, with women being allowed to go to the doctor or pick up their children. "And if you don't do it, there are consequences."

The immigration status of workers has exacerbated the problems, said a former Sanderson worker, Pablo Hernandez, also a pseudonym for privacy. Through an interpreter, Hernandez described managers' treatment of immigrant workers before they have authorization to work in the United States.

"They'd get much more production out of these people, because they were in the country illegally, so they were more vulnerable," he said.

In December 2017, Garcia, Morales, and a few others traveled to Washington, D.C., to meet with officials from the U.S. Department of Agriculture to confirm the findings about the dire working conditions at poultry plants detailed in a report by the U.S. Government Accountability Office.[1] They also attended the annual National COSH conference outside Baltimore, where they were able to connect with other poultry workers and labor advocates.

Encouraged by those meetings, they returned to Texas and filed an OSHA complaint on behalf of a worker who reported the lack of permission to go to the bathroom and problems with chemicals.

Then OSHA called the worker to follow up on the complaint, Morales said. The local OSHA official told the worker that

Sanderson Farms management said the company's policy allowed for necessary bathroom breaks. Morales and other CDL members knew that no matter what was written in the company policy, it didn't happen in practice. Workers were being denied access to the bathroom when they needed it, which violates OSHA regulations.

In May 2018, Garcia, Morales, and two workers returned to Washington, joining poultry workers from the Western North Carolina Workers' Center for a meeting with officials at OSHA's national headquarters. The workers described the restrictions on bathroom use and the local OSHA office's assertion that the company had an acceptable policy. The officials in OSHA's headquarters told them that the explanation offered by the local office was incorrect. The delegation felt vindicated.

But in June, CDL received information from the local OSHA office. It restated the claim from Sanderson Farms that there were no problems—not with bathrooms, not with chemicals, not with injuries. The national and local OSHA offices were clearly at odds.

The company and their lawyers had responded to the complaint, Plankey-Videla said, asserting to OSHA that the company met all chemical and other standards. At the time, Plankey-Videla, an associate professor of sociology at Texas A&M, was on CDL's board of directors.

"We wrote a letter back to OSHA breaking down every single point," Plankey-Videla said, and copied the officials they had met in Washington as well as U.S. Rep. Rosa DeLauro, ranking member of the House Agriculture Appropriations Subcommittee. CDL included photos of labels on boxes showing weights of seventy-seven pounds, which is higher than the limit recommended for safe lifting by the U.S. National Institute for Occupational Safety and Health. CDL also sent a photograph of a document, blank except for a worker's signature on the bottom, typical of ones used to "prove" that the worker had been trained in safety measures.

CDL's letter to OSHA headquarters asked for an unannounced inspection at Sanderson Farms.

A few months later, in late September, an OSHA investigator spent four hours with workers, meeting at St. Teresa Catholic Church in Bryan, Texas. The workers, "point by point, talked about the chemicals, about the various forms of wage theft, about the egregious misuse of FMLA, and the way in which workers had work injuries that were written down as personal problems," Plankey-Videla said.

All of that set the stage for the protest in October 2018. Activists and former employees, among them Hernandez, gathered outside the plant, wearing adult diapers. They carried homemade signs that read, for example, "El Bano Por Favor" (Toilet Please) and "El Pollo en Mi Plato Sabe Mejor con Justicia" (The Chicken on My Plate Tastes Better with Justice).

Poultry workers arriving for the morning shift drove past the demonstration. Some, glad to see the scene, used their cell phones to capture it on video. Others drove straight by, not making any eye contact. A few big rig drivers, hauling massive crates of live chickens, honked and waved.

Along with the diaper-clad protesters, Nora Morales, Nancy Plankey-Videla, Martha Ojeda, Rev. Trent Williams with Friends Congregational Church, and Alex Galimberti of Oxfam America drove through the plant gate to hand deliver a letter to the manager. The letter, addressed to Joe Sanderson Jr., CEO of Sanderson Farms, described problems at the plant including access to the bathroom, exposure to chemicals, and sexual harassment.

Mike Cockrell, Sanderson's chief financial officer, denied allegations of harassment and mistreatment, including the complaints about not being allowed to go to the bathroom.

"Such allegations, they're frankly offensive," Cockrell told a reporter from KBTX, a local television station covering the protest. "The idea that anyone would treat another human being like that is difficult to imagine and if that happened in our plant those supervisors would be terminated immediately."[2]

After the protest, conditions improved immediately at the plant.

"In my opinion, the protest worked, because there were changes," said Hernandez, whose wife was still working at the plant in December 2018. Hernandez's wife told him that a supervisor actually stops by her work station to see if she needs to use the bathroom.

Since the protest, Garcia and Morales heard from a worker who told them that "before they were in hell; now they are in paradise," able to use the bathroom more frequently. Also, workers no longer have to pay for new protective gear if theirs is ripped or unusable.

Those are the kind of wins that keep Garcia and Morales going in a struggle that so often seems daunting.

At the same time, the CDL's financial condition also improved. Through donations and grants, they had enough money to fund more hours for the part-time staffers and to cover the rent—now for the entire store, since the beauty salon has gone out of business. Workers' rights posters covered the salon's wall of mirrors. The local library was renovated, so the CDL snagged the discarded tables, chairs, and a reception desk.

These days, CDL is looking to build committees within the plant to keep up the momentum. What members have noticed over the years is that conditions improve for a time after the protests, but then revert back. The committees are also pressing for more reforms, particularly to issues involving the FMLA. A growing concern is the use of robots in the plant and the impact it has on line speed.

"And in the deboning department, that's where they have a lot of problems with line speed. They brought a robot in, and now everything is going faster because the robot is doing the work of four people," Garcia said, adding that workers are losing their jobs, and those that remain "are having to work harder and their hands are more swollen because of the faster speed."

With or without robots, line speed is an issue. Workers want OSHA to regulate line speeds, but the speed of the line is actually in the U.S. Department of Agriculture's domain, determined by how quickly government inspectors can check the birds' carcasses.

Even so, line speeds tend to creep up. "It's never at the speed that, by law, it should be," Morales said. "It's always higher."

Morales said, "The committees will supervise that things are going well, and in case they are not, they themselves can begin to make changes inside the plant. They are going to be their own leaders; we are just supporting them."

The OSHA inspection spurred by the worker's complaint resulted in two citations against Sanderson Farms for failing to provide appropriate protective gear. The company contested OSHA's findings and a proposed $14,227 in penalties.[3]

"A while back, I felt very frustrated with everything going on, and I was at the point of saying, 'I stop here,'" Garcia said in December 2018. "But we had a meeting with the workers and a worker came who barely speaks [at all] and she was afraid to ask for permission to go to the bathroom. And that day, she told her supervisor, 'I'm going to the bathroom. It's my right.'

"And so, that motivated me and tells me that I'm doing a good job empowering workers."

Nora Morales draws her strength from the stories.

"When CDL was being formed and we started working with people from the poultry plant, what affected me most was realizing that your dignity as a person is being stepped on in such a way that people are abused so much that they start seeing it as normal.

"That's not right."

16

BUTTERFLIES AND BARBED WIRE

The Dutton-Goldfield winery's sun umbrellas on California Highway 116 pointed toward the town of Graton, population 1,700. At 7 a.m. Graton's two-block main street was nearly deserted; the Willow Wood Market Café and Underwood Bar and Bistro were not yet open. They cater to tourists on vineyard tours and wine tastings in Sonoma County.

A block and a world away from Graton's upscale main street was a cheerful one-story building painted mint green. The look was California—flowering trees, colorful landscaping, and a wooden deck with a picnic table. But, instead of a poster advertising the newest chardonnay, a ten-foot-high pumpkin-colored sign at the driveway announced, in big, bold letters: Centro Laboral de Graton, Graton Day Labor Center.

There was pride in the sign, and it seemed to say, "You've arrived."

If early morning in downtown Graton tended toward tranquility, the atmosphere inside the Centro Laboral de Graton (CLG) was anything but *tranquilo* one average Tuesday morning in June 2019.

Already, on that day, names of ten men looking for work were written on the whiteboard by the front desk. Mario Solano and his colleague, both members of CLG's four-person staff, fielded phone calls from employers looking to hire day laborers for landscaping and hauling jobs. There's a separate procedure for domestic workers.

For fifteen years, the CLG, with five hundred members—day laborers and domestic workers from Sonoma County—has offered employers the opportunity to hire its members through a process that is democratic, fair, and transparent for both parties. Even though day laborers still hustle work on a corner just a few blocks away, their numbers have diminished.

CLG members make all operational decisions, from setting annual dues of $60 to establishing the hourly wages employers must agree to pay depending on the job. Members also choose topics for skills development workshops and set priorities for local and state civic activities. Lately, the emphasis has been on immigration rights and wage theft. Decisions follow discussions during weekly member assemblies.

On that Tuesday, as a few workers crowded near the desks to register for the day's jobs by writing their names and membership numbers in the ledger, Solano maintained the daily list of workers in order of who first queued up for available jobs—matching workers with jobs scheduled in advance by employers while also dealing with new requests.

The ins and outs of the hiring list are part of CLG's Acuerdos y Procesos. The agreements and processes are the written procedures passed yearly by CLG's general assembly. The preface of the nine-page document, written in both English and Spanish, reads: "We establish these agreements so that there may be a center that advances justice, liberty and dignity," with the purpose of creating "comradery based on unity."

Solano's job is to make sure the procedures are followed. "It's crazy," he said, taking a break. "People from other worker centers have come to learn our process. It's very complicated and hard to learn."

Because it was a Tuesday, a few men in work clothes began moving chairs into a large circle in preparation for the weekly assembly, held at 8:15 a.m. before jobs are dispatched at 8:45 a.m.

A flip chart in the front of the room read "Asamblea" (Assembly). It was the meeting agenda. By 8:15, about twenty workers were sitting around the circle. Deysi Lopez, a CLG member, was waiting to preside over the meeting. Originally from Oaxaca, Mexico, Lopez joined the worker center three years ago. She previously worked in the fields, but now gets jobs through the worker center. She had her name on the day's hiring list.

At the top of the agenda was "Conozca sus derechos acerca del ICE" (Know your rights on the Immigration and Customs Enforcement agency).

Christy Lubin, CLG's executive director, asked, "What have you heard on the news about threats against immigrants? What did President Trump announce?"[1] Several men replied, "radadas" (raids). Questions and answers flew back and forth in Spanish.

Another worker said: "ICE will be ready to go into stores, laundromats, they will have free rein to go anywhere they want to do the raids."

Lubin probed the group, "Does ICE have the right to do these raids?"

"No," some said in unison.

A man wearing a beige baseball cap said, "Maybe if you are in public, but not on private property." The men standing near him looked unsure about his answer.

"ICE does not have the authority to force someone out of their car, off of the street, from their house, without an arrest warrant," Lubin explained. "There is a lot of fear about the raids; people are living in fear. What can we do?"

A member chimed in, "We can become informed, organize ourselves, educate ourselves."

"Yes, at a minimum, we should educate ourselves about our rights," Lubin said.

Lubin and Lopez each held up bright red business cards.

"We are going to go through the most important points," Lubin explained. Lopez had already listed each on a flip chart.

"ICE cannot go into your home without a warrant for your arrest for deportation. Do not open your door. Let them know that they can pass the paperwork under your door. If the paper does not have correct information about you, or it's not signed, then it is not valid," Lubin said, emphasizing each point.

To reinforce the lesson, Lubin and Lopez decided to act out a scene. Lopez played an immigrant woman in her home; Lubin played the ICE agent.

"Knock, knock, knock," Lubin said, pretending to knock on a door. "Open the door. I am from ICE."

Lopez looked startled and took a breath to stay calm. She went to the pretend door, but didn't open it. Lubin knocked more loudly: "Open the door. It's ICE. I have a deportation order."

"Pass the information under the door," Lopez said.

Lubin slid the make-believe document under the make-believe door. Lopez looked it over. She saw it was not valid. She slid the document back under the door. With confidence, she said, "This document is not signed."

Everyone chuckled because Lubin, playing the ICE agent, looked surprised. Lubin picked up the document from the floor, turned, and walked away; the audience applauded.

The skit had a light-hearted feel, but it again turned serious.

Lubin repeated the message, "You should not open your door. Once you open the door, you basically invited them in."

The topic of ICE raids was not new for CLG's worker assembly. Since 2017, immigrants have been the target of the Trump administration, but the hostility peaked days before the Tuesday meeting in June 2019. The president had tweeted, "millions of illegal aliens will be removed as fast as they come in."

The pronouncement provoked anxiety and fear. Ensuring that immigrants know their rights—one of CLG's objectives—can help alleviate those worries. Lubin and Lopez didn't just tell the workers about their rights; they showed them how to exercise them. That was the purpose of the skit—how to respond to that knock on the door.

A worker in the assembly asked, "What should we do if ICE came here? If they came on to this property?"

"We are the owners of this property," Lubin answered. "We don't rent this place. It is private property."

Pointing outside to the shaded deck and picnic table, Lopez reminded the assembly that everyone should come inside the building if ICE comes onto the property. The staff will lock the doors.

"We can stay inside," Lubin added, "and ask ICE to show us any orders of deportation either under the door or through the window."

Lopez and Lubin grabbed a handful of red business cards that had been stacked up on a bookshelf. Lopez handed her pile off to the young man wearing the beige baseball cap. He took one and passed along the stack.

With English on one side and Spanish on the other, the cards repeat the lesson. They list the rights and protections for individuals under the U.S. Constitution. They apply to all people in the United States, regardless of their immigration status.

The first line on the card reads, "I am exercising my 5th Amendment rights under the U.S. Constitution to remain silent." Another line advises not to let an immigration agent or the police enter the home without a valid warrant."

Lopez reminded the group to remain silent if approached by ICE; just hand them this card. "Take a few," she said. "Give them to your family and friends."

One member advised the others to make sure their children know these procedures. Otherwise, if they hear a knock at the door, most kids will just open it.

The red business cards were designed by the Immigrant Legal Resource Center, a national nonprofit organization that promotes and defends immigrant rights. They have templates for the cards in eight languages. They are formatted to be downloaded and printed. Immigrant rights groups and worker centers have been printing thousands of them. CLG and other worker centers are key to distributing them in communities across the country.

A woman who was standing near the back of the group spoke up. Her voice trembled. She has friends, she said, who are afraid of being pulled over on the freeway. They wonder what they will do if they are deported to Mexico.

"I told them they should come here to the center and they can learn about their rights," she said.

The assembly nodded in agreement.

Lopez pointed to the next item on the assembly's agenda. CLG and the California Labor Commissioner's Office were organizing a wage theft clinic. The commissioner's office planned to have at least five lawyers available at the clinic to help people file claims to recover their wages.

"If you know anyone who didn't get paid at all or didn't get paid the wage the employer promised, that's wage theft," Lubin said. "And when you work more than eight hours and aren't paid overtime, and when you don't get your breaks, that's wage theft."

Because CLG has a process to match workers with employers, its members are less likely to be victims of wage theft. But the problem is pervasive, especially for people of color, immigrants, and those who work in low-wage jobs.

"This wage theft clinic is a pilot with the labor commissioner," she said. "Tell your family and neighbors about it."

Deysi Lopez moved over to a section on the whiteboard that read "Voluntarios Dia de Trabajo." It was a list of members who had already volunteered to help with a workday on the upcoming Sunday. The center relies on the membership to clean and maintain their meeting space and the building grounds. There is weeding to do and some tending of the vegetable garden.

Lopez held the blue magic marker in her hand. "We'll have

coffee and donuts," Lubin added. Lopez added a couple more names to the list.

The last item was marked off the assembly's agenda. Lopez adjourned the meeting with a slow clap of her hands. Everyone joined in and the clapping got faster and louder until it sounded like applause.

It was time for the day's jobs to be dispatched.

By noon, all available jobs had been assigned. The names of three day laborers were on the whiteboard under the heading "Pendiente" (Pending)—for priority the next day. Mario Solano, one of the job dispatchers, took time for a lunch break. He sat at the picnic table on the building's wooden deck. It was a quiet spot in a place that's been important to Mario Solano since 2007.

In 1999, Solano was living in Mexico and studying to be a biologist. The prospect of ending up a school biology teacher wasn't appealing. He left Mexico to live with his brother who was working in the San Francisco area. Construction companies were hiring; Solano started at the bottom as a general laborer. Within a year, "they were training me to do all different things," Solano explained. "I was also taking English classes and earned my ESL certification."

The 2007 financial crisis and recession walloped Northern California's construction industry. Solano lost his job. That's when his personal experience with CLG began.

"It was like you saw today," Solano said, "with all the workers coming here and getting on the list for jobs."

But the economy was in a slump. On the days Solano wasn't dispatched for a job, he still spent time at the worker center.

"When I was here, I would just go up front and tell the guy, 'Hey, do you need any help with anything?'" Solano was an eager volunteer, which led to part-time work at the center—first to open the doors on Sundays for worker dispatch, and then to back up the Saturday dispatcher.

"I just got more and more involved. I became a full-time staff member, forty hours per week. I did that for about five years."

Solano's construction skills served him well in 2012 when CLG didn't have funding any longer for his position. With five years at the center, he had developed his own relationships with employers. One job would snowball into another. "Employers would refer me to other employers. For seven years, I had all of my own bosses, doing my own thing," he said. "If I felt like working ten hours a day or twelve hours a day, I could, or set my own schedule."

In early 2018, CLG had a staff position available. Executive Director Lubin asked Solano if he was interested in coming back. "I was so busy with my jobs and it took me a few months to decide," Solano said.

He thought he would miss working outdoors and the physical nature of carpentry and repair jobs. He accepted the CLG position, but added, "I saved all my tools. I can still do that work when I want to."

Watching Solano interact with the day laborers shows that his tools go beyond hammers and battery-powered drills. He's been a construction worker. He's been on CLG's hiring list. He understands the jobs that employers want done. He sees, too, that the worker center can be more than a place to get a job for the day.

"If a worker goes out and the employer feels comfortable with him, they can establish their own relationship," Solano said. "When an employer comes to the center, we tell them right away, 'You know, if you're happy with this person, you are welcome to hire him back.'"

The written agreement and processes developed by CLG members includes the hourly wage charge to employers for dozens of tasks. Mowing grass and weeding, for example, costs $15 per hour, ditch-digging costs $18 per hour, masonry work costs $20 per hour. Different rates are charged depending on whether the worker uses his own equipment or the employers'. Each year, the general assembly reviews and, if necessary, revises the wage list.

When a member gets a job booked through CLG, the employer agrees to pay the hourly rate set by the membership. The worker is paid the full amount directly by the employer. CLG doesn't take a percentage of the wage paid. The worker doesn't pay CLG a referral fee.

"If we lose a worker because they make their own connections with employers and they are doing their own thing, that is a success for us," Solano said. He speaks from experience.

Solano didn't become a biology teacher, but coaching and teaching are part of his nature. He takes time to get to know the workers who come to CLG, and they get to know him. "I let them know that I was in their position when I first came here," Solano explained. "I tell them, 'I started getting jobs here. I made my own connections and now I have my own employers. I have my own bosses. This can be you.'"

Even when a CLG member fosters a personal relationship with an employer, the CLG's wage scale stands, although there are exceptions. "Sometimes an employer will explain that he can't pay $25 per hour, but 'I can give you five days of work per week.' He might say he can't pay $25 per hour, but can pay $22," Solano said. "If the worker agrees to that, it's fine. [He will be] working five days a week for $22 an hour rather than coming here and just going out as jobs are available."

His face brightened. "That's what we want. We help to make that first connection."

As a construction laborer, Solano didn't know he'd find himself on a trajectory to leadership at the CLG.

"They gave me the tools and I started implementing them," he said.

Solano's leadership has gone beyond the mint-colored walls of the CLG, as its members build bridges—and support—in the larger Sonoma County community.

"When I first started coming here," Solano said, "there were people, especially some seniors and women, who were afraid of hiring a Latino guy to work on their house. It was very common. We would get calls every day, 'I don't want a person that looks different from me to work on my place.'

"The community didn't trust us," he said.

"I'm most proud of the change we have seen in the community towards the labor center," Solano said. "They are really comfortable and happy with us."

And for that Solano credits the CLG.

"This is a center of opportunity. You get the support that you need in this worker center that you won't get anywhere else. They give you the tools to go out there and be somebody," he said, "and protect yourself by knowing your rights."

Solano finished his lunch and walked back inside.

There he saw the same posters that hung in the meeting room. Translated from Spanish, one read, "Labor Rights for All." Another reads: "Equality for All, Nothing More, Nothing Less."

But given the topic of the day's *asamblea*, probably no poster was more meaningful than the one showing a stream of monarch butterflies drifting through a crystal-clear blue sky, across barbed wire. The beautiful winged creatures, which fly three thousand miles north from Mexico each spring, are an important symbol of hope to immigrants.

The message on the poster with its blue sky, butterflies, and barbed wire?

"Ain't no border high enough. Migration is a human right."

Milagros Barreto, organizer, MassCOSH, Boston. *I. George Bilyk*

Magdalena Zylinska, member, Arise Chicago. *I. George Bilyk*

Part V

The Fruits of Their Labors

Around the nation, worker centers represent many kinds of workers—people who work in homes, on construction sites and dairy farms, in poultry processing plants, in warehouses, and in garment factories. They are Latino, Filipino, Black, Polish, and Somalian. Some are undocumented, some are citizens. As different as they are, their challenges are similar. Wage theft abounds for many of them. Employed by temporary agencies, some workers find themselves working without pay in unsafe conditions. Housekeepers face the same challenges, exacerbated by working in isolation. Awakening the labor movement, worker centers and their members are joining together to build and protect the power of workers. They have stories about their paths to victories through collective action.

> It's great to pass laws, but if we don't enforce them, what's the point, because we know employers don't follow the law.
> —Shelly Ruzicka, Arise Chicago

> That is the power of enforcement.
> —Rebecca Fuentes, former lead organizer, Workers' Center of Central New York

17

BEYOND THE BROOM, BREAKING BARRIERS

If there is any effort that exemplifies all that worker centers are and all that they can be, it's the combined campaign of worker centers to build power for nannies, housekeepers, and caregivers. In states around the nation—Massachusetts, Illinois, New Jersey, New York, California—laws are being enacted to guarantee wages and better working conditions for domestic workers.

The energy on the state level feeds off a national push to accomplish the same aims, with efforts led by the National Domestic Workers Alliance (NDWA), an organization representing hundreds of thousands of workers. The spirit of the campaign—built by marches, rallies, and protests—has gone beyond strategy sessions over stale coffee to capture the public imagination, so much so that *Roma*, a movie about a housekeeper in Mexico City, won three Oscars in 2019.

No wonder Rosa Sanluis and Terry Villasenor traded their practical work shoes for glamorous high heels and evening gowns. It was February 2019 in Hollywood, California, and the two domestic workers were walking the red carpet, side by side with Eva Longoria, Rashida Jones, Natalie Portman, and other A-listers. Sanluis, from New York, and Villasenor, from Florida, joined dozens of other members of the NDWA at Oscar-night events. They were guests of the celebrities and ready to savor the Academy Award wins for *Roma*.[1]

Photos on the red carpet and dazzling after-parties were not goals that inspired the housekeepers, nannies, and home care aides when they first set out to improve their working conditions. Even so, the momentous night in Hollywood wouldn't have happened if not for two decades of organizing. Domestic workers in the United States have developed into leaders of a new labor movement—one that relies on worker strength, often independent of traditional unions.

Domestic workers aren't covered by the Fair Labor Standards Act or the National Labor Relations Act, federal laws dating back to the 1930s that mandate minimum wages, overtime pay, hours of work, and the right to form unions. Lawmakers excluded domestic and farmworkers at the insistence of southern Democrats who wanted to maintain the racial and economic order rooted in slavery.

The nation's 2.5 million domestic workers are overwhelmingly immigrant women and women of color. Their workplaces are hidden behind people's front doors. Their responsibilities in people's homes are personal and intimate: being a companion to an elderly person, bathing and dressing children or the infirm, cleaning bedrooms and bathrooms, witnessing family arguments and dysfunction. There are no co-workers to confide in. And, although they may hear they are "part of the family," domestic workers are employees.

But despite this inequity in labor law—or perhaps because of it—they exemplify a new model of worker organizing. From behind their mops, strollers, and bedside trays, they have served as an empowering example to other marginalized workers.

"We're hoping that what we're doing motivates other low-wage workers to organize, too," said Linda Burnham, NDWA's research director. "Each sector of the labor force has issues and circumstances unique to what they do, but we absolutely feel like the work we're doing in fighting for domestic workers is part of a larger attempt to really figure out how, in this economic environment, low-wage workers can get a better deal."

Ai-jen Poo, NDWA's executive director, credits the movement's roots in part to two Asian community organizations in New York City created long before there was a National Domestic Workers Alliance or movies about housekeepers.

During the 1990s, the Organizing Asian Communities (CAAAV) and the Organizing South Asian Workers (Andolan) were helping domestic workers address unpaid wages and discrimination, but their existing constituencies were relatively small.[2] To expand their influence, CAAAV and Andolan reached out to the much larger community of Caribbean and Latina women who were also domestic workers in New York City. An estimated 200,000 domestic workers were employed in the city at the time.

Together, the women conducted surveys of other domestic workers to assemble data on their job responsibilities, hours of work, wages, benefits, and other employment conditions. They created a new organization called Domestic Workers United (DWU), where Ai-jen Poo served as the lead organizer. DWU's methodology, particularly the use of a survey, became the prototype for the organizing that followed nationwide years later, not only for domestic workers, but for marginalized workers in many fields, from construction to farming.

"Right now, it's like the wild, wild West—anything goes," she told the *New York Times* in 2008, talking about the situation for nannies, housekeepers, and caregivers. "Our point is that there needs to be a basic standard of protections, because the majority fall under employers who abuse, and everyone is vulnerable."[3]

DWU teamed up with Damayan Migrant Workers Association, Haitian Women for Haitian Refugees, Adhikaar, and other immigrant rights groups to push the New York City Council to address the needs of housekeepers and nannies. In 2003—in a 49–0 vote—the city council mandated that placement agencies inform domestic workers about their rights. The ordinance also required employers who hire domestic workers to provide a written statement of the employee's rights and the employer's responsibilities.[4] At the time, the law was considered the most far-reaching one in the United States for domestic workers.

Outside of New York City, domestic worker organizations in Los Angeles, Oakland, San Francisco, and other cities began networking. In 2007, fifty domestic workers from thirteen organizations convened in Atlanta as part of the United States Social Forum. They were women who had emigrated from Bangladesh, Haiti, Mexico, the Philippines, and other countries. They were representing groups such as CASA de Maryland, the Coalition for Humane Immigrant Rights of Los Angeles, Mujeres Unidas y Activas, and the Women's Collective of La Raza Centro Legal.[5] Over four days, they shared stories and learned from each other. Their vision was (and remains) achieving dignity and justice for domestic workers. At the forum, the thirteen groups voted to establish the National Domestic Workers Alliance. They left the event on a high.

Reflecting on this milestone, some of the organizers wrote, "across language barriers and cultural divides, women shared experiences about organizing in our corners of the country, laughed and cried together, and developed lasting relationships."[6]

Returning home, the worker leaders in New York ramped up their efforts to pass a statewide domestic workers bill of rights. They adopted three messages that helped build relationships with women's equality groups, civil rights organizations, unions, the faith community, and employers: "Respect the work that makes all other work possible"; "Reverse a long history of discrimination and exclusion," and "Standards benefit everyone."[7]

Their campaign for the nation's first statewide Domestic Workers' Bill of Rights lasted six years. Domestic Workers United in New York made certain that lawmakers and the public heard their stories and their demands for labor protections. The bill they pushed included the right to overtime pay after forty hours of work in a week; a twenty-four-hour rest day every seven days; three days of paid leave after one year of work for the same employer;

and legal protections against sexual and racial harassment. The legislature passed the bill in July 2010 and it was signed by New York governor David Paterson.

The *New York Times* reported the event, writing: "The passage was met with peals of laughter and applause from a group of domestic workers who traveled to Albany to witness the vote. As they filed out of the Senate gallery on Thursday, some of the workers cried, while others hugged, took photos on their cellphones or called friends with the good news."[8]

As the Empire State's campaign was progressing, the NDWA, borrowing a leaf from New York's playbook, made plans for a national survey.

Why? Because one of the first steps of successful worker organizing is having information on who makes up a particular workforce, their concerns, experiences, and priorities. Considering the isolating nature of domestic work, gathering such information is a challenge. NDWA aimed to fill that data gap, launching a national survey effort and eventually providing what might be the clearest picture to date of the experience of domestic workers in the United States. The alliance partnered with local worker centers around the country to gather information, with members of Fe y Justicia Worker Center leading the survey effort in Houston.

But before getting any information, organizers had to lay the groundwork. First came the training about the survey, next came practicing techniques to encourage domestic workers to participate, then came the legwork. In Houston, 150 domestic workers completed the survey and what they reported mirrored survey findings across the nation. Domestic workers routinely experienced wage theft and disrespect, the survey showed.

The survey revealed that domestic workers face a variety of preventable workplace hazards that can result in injury and illness. For example, Laura Perez-Boston, Fe y Justicia's executive director at the time, was surprised by how many surveyed workers reported respiratory problems. And because many domestic workers don't have time in their work schedules to see a doctor and don't have paid time off, they are often forced to ignore their health problems. Many accept work-related health problems as simply part of the job.

The survey responses collected in Houston and elsewhere eventually became part of *Home Economics: The Invisible and Unregulated World of Domestic Work*, which NDWA released in 2012.[9] The report's findings were based on nearly 2,100 surveys of domestic workers collected by about three dozen community groups in fourteen U.S. metropolitan areas.

"Women's work has been undervalued probably since the beginning of time, and racism is still alive and well," Perez-Boston said. "And because it's done primarily by women of color, there isn't a lot of consideration for their full range of human needs. Sometimes, it isn't even considered a real job."

NDWA's *Home Economics* pulled back the curtain on the conditions and experiences domestic workers face, documenting issues such as wage exploitation, preventable on-the-job injuries, and the little—if any—power domestic workers have in improving their work environments and holding employers accountable.

Bringing visibility to the employment conditions of domestic workers was a key aim of the NDWA's *Home Economics* report. The report confirmed that working in people's homes creates an atmosphere ripe for problems and exploitation. The survey data illustrated widespread substandard work environments, poor wages, and hazardous work conditions: 23 percent of workers were paid below state minimum wage, 70 percent were paid less than $13 per hour, and the median hourly wage was $6.15, more than a dollar below the $7.25 hourly federal minimum wage at the time. Sixty-five percent of domestic workers surveyed did not have health insurance, and only 4 percent received employer-provided health insurance.

"Although the work they do is so important, it's done behind closed doors," said NDWA's deputy director Mariana Viturro.

"The survey can help build recognition that domestic workers deserve the same protections that all workers have."

The survey helped fill a critical data gap, but also assisted allies to connect with other domestic workers and build their ranks. "Learning about their needs and conditions will ensure that any legislative changes that we win are really at the heart of what domestic workers have defined that they need," Viturro said.

Perez-Boston agreed. "Not only was it a good tool to produce a powerful report with hard data that show the accumulation of stories we've been hearing for years, but it was also a very empowering process for the workers themselves," she said. "It helped bring workers together to talk about the most common issues they're facing and their priorities for creating change." [10]

Bringing workers together—before and after the survey—helped build campaigns in states around the nation.

In California, the Household Workers Coalition—now called the California Domestic Workers Coalition—was engaged in its own fight for a bill of rights.

By the time the domestic worker groups had gathered in Atlanta for the 2006 United States Social Forum, California's Domestic Workers Coalition had already lost a legislative battle. In 2006, Republican governor Arnold Schwarzenegger vetoed the coalition-backed Household Worker Bill of Rights. The domestic workers persevered and advanced their efforts with research. The Women's Collective of La Raza Centro Legal and Mujeres Unidas y Activas collaborated with the San Francisco Department of Health to investigate employment conditions for domestic workers.[11]

When California governor Jerry Brown took office in 2011, domestic worker groups were hopeful their bill would finally become law. But the Democratic governor vetoed the bill when it landed on his desk in 2012, persuaded by opposition from the California Chamber of Commerce and businesses that provide home care aides. It was a blow to the movement. Domestic workers, unions, and allies in-state and nationwide were surprised and disappointed—but never deterred.

In 2013, a modified version of the bill passed and Brown signed it. Now, caregivers, nannies, housecleaners, and other household workers—an estimated 300,000 in the state—are no longer excluded from overtime time pay or workers' compensation for job-related injuries. Their employers are required to provide written information on how much and when the domestic worker will be paid, and the rate can be no less than California's or the locality's minimum wage, whichever is higher.

"This has been a really long struggle," said Maria Distancia, a member of the California Domestic Workers Coalition. "We've been fighting since 2006," she told *In These Times*. "We're out of the shadows now," Distancia, a nanny who lives in Oakland, added. "We're becoming more visible." [12]

It was also 2013 when the Illinois Domestic Workers Coalition kicked into high gear. Over three and a half years, the Latino Union of Chicago, Arise Chicago, Alliance of Filipinos for Immigrant Rights and Empowerment (AFIRE Chicago), and the Service Employees International Union made their voices heard and their demands clear. They spoke at the state capital, in churches, and with college students. They held banners high at labor rallies and marches for immigrant rights. A 2016 bill adopted by lawmakers expanded on provisions contained in the other states' laws. It also mandated that employers provide live-in domestic workers at least twenty-four hours of rest per week.

Campaigns by nannies, housecleaners, and other household workers have resulted in labor protections in Hawaii (2013), Massachusetts (2014), Connecticut (2015), Oregon (2015), Nevada (2017), New Mexico (2018), and the cities of Seattle (2018) and Philadelphia (2019). Some create parity with employment rights provided to all other workers in the state, while others are modest, but still meaningful.

Iamê Manucci, the daughter of a domestic worker, celebrated

an amendment to a Connecticut law. It was not a full-blown bill of rights, but deleting just three words, "excluding domestic service," made minimum wage and overtime protections applicable to domestic workers in the state. Manucci, who ran the campaign in Connecticut, said the change was finally an acknowledgment that people who labor in another's home are indeed employees. It's "the recognition that you have the dignity every other worker has, that you exist—by law," she said.[13]

For most domestic workers, the dollars they earn making beds and changing diapers help them support families in the United States and in their home countries. Standing up for their rights carries risks. Yet they persevere, sticking with the struggle as months and years pass.

That's how it worked for housekeeper Magdalena Zylinska, an immigrant from Poland and a worker leader at Arise Chicago. She remembered crying for joy when Illinois passed its domestic worker protection bill in 2016.

"Sometimes you have to break some barriers," Zylinska said, "and just go on and do the right thing and hope other people follow."

Thanks to domestic workers, they have.

18

TEMPORARY JOB,
PERMANENT STRUGGLE

Juan Calderas broke two discs in his back while working at a Massachusetts fruit processing company. The job was rough. "We had no breaks, until after ten hours of work. I was carrying a large bucket of fruit and fell," he explained. "When the employer refused to pay my doctor's bills, that's when I learned that I wasn't working for the company at all, but instead for a temporary agency."[1]

In Illinois, at the Great Kitchens food prep plant, Marcela Gallegos and co-workers were also temp workers. Their job was folding eighty pizza boxes per minute, and if they didn't keep up, the uncooked pizzas would pile up. Her aching hands kept her up at night and a painful ganglion cyst emerged on the wrist of her right hand. Gallegos, in her thirties, knew it wasn't going to be easy getting medical treatment. A co-worker had similar symptoms and told her supervisor about them. The supervisor said it wasn't Great Kitchen's responsibility. Gallegos and the others worked for Staffing Network, and if someone got hurt it was the temp agency's problem.

But whose problem is it, really?

That's the dilemma temporary workers face. Who is supposed to pay them? Who is supposed to handle injuries on the job? Who is supposed to make sure they have the safety equipment and training they need? If there are discrimination and harassment issues, where should they turn?

Millions of U.S. workers—16 million in 2019—are employed in "temp jobs" through the staffing industry.[2] Since the Great Recession of 2008, it's been one of the fastest-growing sectors of the economy. Temp workers give businesses flexibility to make "just in time" production easier, allowing them to expand and contract their workforces in response to market demands. But the employment model has downsides for workers, from lack of transparency about who they work for, to firms using "temps" to skirt worker rights or to evade labor laws outright.

After getting injured and then the run-around about who was going to pay their doctor bills, Gallegos in Illinois and Calderas in Massachusetts joined worker centers to get help. Grateful, and galvanized by what they learned in the process, Gallegos and Calderas became leaders in statewide campaigns to expand the rights of temp workers.

Across the nation, from Massachusetts to California, from Illinois to New Jersey, worker centers have become the agents of change in temporary staffing, pushing for new legislation for stronger protection for temp workers. That's because, in many cases, their members—often immigrant non-English speakers desperate for a paycheck—turn to staffing agencies for work. In turn, the staffing agencies need these workers to unload fruit, fold pizza boxes, and sort orders at warehouses. For the staffing agencies, the people are the product, bodies to slide into slots to fill requisitions from businesses.

It's a situation that lends itself to abuse.

In most states, there is no legal requirement for temp agencies to tell workers *where* they are going to work, exactly *what* they will be asked to do, or *how long* the shift will be. And even beyond those basics, there's no guarantee that the temporary jobs will at any point become permanent, giving the workers the stability they need to pursue the American dream, however limited.

Different worker centers used different tactics to move ahead on the issue. The Immigrant Worker Center at the Massachusetts

Coalition for Occupational Safety and Health (MassCOSH) started with surveys and focus groups. In Illinois, groundbreaking work by journalists accelerated the process being pushed by a coalition of worker centers. And in New Jersey, New Labor sent its future executive director out to temp agencies to gain on-the-job expertise. Each group took note of the successes of the others, incorporating those wins in their campaigns, aiming to create ever stronger protections for workers.

Surveys by MassCOSH found that temp workers were employed in low-paying jobs, and in particularly hazardous industries, such as construction, recycling, fish processing, and waste hauling. They were routinely expected to pay for safety equipment, and fees were deducted from their paychecks to cover transportation to the assigned worksite.[3]

"We conducted focus groups to see if these were isolated incidents," said Isabel Lopez, who was coordinator at the time of MassCOSH's Immigrant Worker Center. "We found that more than fifty workers—in different temp agencies from Lawrence to New Bedford to Chelsea—had very similar situations."[4]

While temp work is sometimes described as a stepping-stone to full-time employment, this is often not the case, even when an employer has an ongoing, consistent job to fill. "Temp is often a misnomer," said Marcy Goldstein-Gelb, former executive director of MassCOSH.[5] In their survey, they heard from workers who had job assignments *for years* at the same employer—giving rise to the term "permatemp."[6]

MassCOSH led the REAL (Reform Employment Agency Law) Coalition, a group of forty community, faith, union, and legal organizations, which began in earnest during 2010 to push for a new law to reform practices in the commonwealth's staffing industry. Worker centers in the coalition included the Brazilian Worker Center,[7] Centro Comunitario de los Trabajadores of New Bedford, and the Metrowest Worker Center. Each had members who were temp workers who used their voices and their stories to expose abuses in the industry. Each group in the REAL Coalition targeted lawmakers to urge and then secure support for new protections.

Then tragedy struck.

In December 2011, Daniel Collazo Torres was fatally injured at Tribe Mediterranean Foods, a manufacturing plant in Taunton, Massachusetts. Torres, twenty-eight, a temp worker, was crushed in an industrial grinder used to make hummus. When the U.S. Occupational Safety and Health Administration (OSHA) announced citations six months later against Tribe Mediterranean Foods, the REAL Coalition used the news to further highlight the need for better protections for temp workers.

"The temp agency industry is just not regulated in our state," Goldstein-Gelb told a reporter with the *Taunton Daily Gazette.* "They need to be cognizant of the hazards their current employees are involved with," adding that the bill being considered by lawmakers would make sure temp workers don't fall through the cracks and become victims of labor violations.[8]

Within months, the commonwealth's House and Senate passed the Temporary Workers Right to Know Act. Governor Deval Patrick signed it into law in August 2012 and it took effect on January 31, 2013. Staffing agencies in Massachusetts are now required to provide workers with a written job order including details rarely provided previously.

Importantly, the job order must specify the actual name of the temporary agency as well as its owners. This was in response to problems government investigators had in tracking down company principles to pay employees in wage theft cases. The written job order also must include when and how much the worker will be paid, and any fees the worker will be charged, such as for meals or transportation. It must list any special clothing, tools, and trainings necessary for the job. The law also prohibits staffing agencies from charging a worker for getting a work assignment, criminal background checks, or drug testing, as well as for transportation the agency requires the worker to use.

Marcy Goldstein-Gelb stood next to Governor Patrick at the bill signing, but a victory one day begins a new campaign the next.

"A bill is simply a piece of paper," said Monica Halas, a member of the REAL Coalition and attorney with the Greater Boston Legal Services, "unless those who are affected know about their rights and these rights are protected by strong regulatory and enforcement provisions."[9]

On the day the law took effect, the coalition ramped up its awareness campaign. A van-load of workers and community members set out on a daylong "Temp Workers Ride to Know." They started their statewide excursion with an early morning stop at a Labor Ready office in Lawrence, Massachusetts. They passed out sample job orders to temp workers so they'd know what the new law requires, and they spoke to the staffing agency management to ensure they knew what is expected under the law.

"This law is so important," said Soledad Araque, a member of the Immigrant Worker Center at MassCOSH. "I worked for a temp agency and didn't get paid all my wages, was charged $3 every day for transportation and got no information about my job. This law will make a huge difference in protecting workers."[10]

While Araque, Juan Calderas, and others in the REAL Coalition were leafleting temp workers about their new rights, Marcela Gallegos was fed up with her employer, Staffing Network, and the situation at Great Kitchens in Illinois. She decided to join the Chicago Workers' Collaborative (CWC), a worker center with a special focus on temp workers. CWC was part of the National Staffing Workers Alliance, a coalition of groups organized in 2012 to put pressure on temp agencies and the businesses that use temp workers.[11]

"Before, this whole industry was operating in the shadows," said Tim Bell, CWC's organizing director and coordinator of the temp worker health and safety program. "Now they're going to have to clean up their act. This is a system that's pushing health and safety standards to the bottom," Bell added. "The idea is to push the liability back on the host employer—that's where the leverage lies."

The temp worker leaders in Chicago and their advocates had high-profile validation not available elsewhere.

In 2013, Michael Grabell, at ProPublica, and Jeff Tyler, with American Public Media, published *Taken for a Ride: Temp Agencies and "Raiteros" in Immigrant Chicago.* Their joint investigation of what they described as the "largely secret underworld of temporary labor in the U.S.," revealed how some of country's largest firms use staffing agencies to man their manufacturing plants and warehouses. Their reporting crossed the country, but they concluded that the epicenter of abuse was in Chicagoland, where labor brokers known as *raiteros* "have melded with temp agencies and their corporate clients in a way that might be unparalleled anywhere in America."[12]

Grabell and Tyler's investigation exposed new ways in which temp workers were being exploited and how their exploitation evolved. Illinois had a law on the books that regulated temporary labor services agencies, and in 2006 additional mandates on the industry were put in place.[13] But the explosion in the industry beginning in 2009—especially pronounced in Chicagoland where distribution centers for goods are situated around seven interstate highways and six railroads—exposed weaknesses in the existing law.[14] CWC and its partners in the National Staffing Workers Alliance wanted more for temp workers than simply right-to-know. The wanted the post-recession economy to provide direct-hire jobs, not one that perpetuated a class of low-wage "permatemps."

Another dirty secret in the industry? Racism based on stereotypes about Black and Latino workers. Rosa Ceja, a former dispatcher for a staffing agency in a Chicago suburb, discovered that host employers use code words—*guapo* and *feo*—to categorize the race of the workers they wanted for a job.

Speaking to reporter Will Evans at the Center for Investigative Reporting, Ceja explained that her fellow recruiters told her that *guapo* meant a Black worker. "Black people didn't want to work hard or get their hands dirty, they explained, so they were called the pretty ones. Latinos, the *feos* or ugly ones, were what the company wanted."[15]

Ceja connected with CWC, whose membership had largely been Latino. However, as CWC began to grasp this further ugliness in the staffing industry, it expanded its outreach. Temp workers—Black, Latino, and white—needed to unite in order to hold temp agencies accountable.

Lawyer Chris Williams, an original founder of the CWC in 2000, began representing Black workers in employment discrimination cases.[16] He sued staffing firms on their behalf through his private practice, called Workers' Law Office, P.C. Williams was familiar with investigations by the Equal Employment Opportunity Commission, which concluded, as did his clients' lawsuits, that some temp agencies were discriminating on the basis of race.

Temp workers, organizing through CWC, Arise Chicago, the Latino Union, Centro de Trabajadores Unidos, and other worker centers, pushed lawmakers in 2014 to amend the Illinois Human Rights Act. The proposed amendment called for temp agencies to use a contact form that allowed the job seeker to self-identify their race and gender, and to submit the data annually to the state Department of Labor. The bill also stipulated that if a host employer failed to investigate suspected discrimination by their staffing agency, the host employer would also be committing a civil rights violation. The bill had one sponsor, Rep. Kenneth Dunkin, and lawmakers debated it in May 2015 in a House committee. However, it languished there, hindered by two forces: industry claims of paperwork nightmares and heated objections from a lawmaker who asserted the law would hurt Latino workers in his district.[17] When the legislative session ended, the bill died in the committee.

The legislative response to Dunkin's bill indicated the campaign was not advancing. So the worker centers ramped up outreach to more lawmakers about the range of abuse suffered by temp workers. The worker centers and their allies talked about harassment and discrimination, and also described how the industry had created a growing class of low-wage "permatemps." Momentum built. By the time the next legislative session commenced, in late January 2017, there was a new and more expansive bill—the Responsible Job Creation Act—and it had thirty-nine sponsors.

During legislative hearings over the next four months, lawmakers heard testimony from 663 proponents. They included dozens of temp workers, including Marcela Gallegos, of CWC, who stuck with the campaign for four years following her injuries at Great Kitchen.

By July 2017, the bill had bipartisan support and was adopted by the Illinois General Assembly by a 108–37 vote. The bill's lead sponsor, Rep. Carol Ammons, thanked lawmakers and said passing the bill "signals to all the temp workers in Illinois that they have support from the Capitol and justice is on its way."[18] Republican governor Bruce Rauner signed the bill into law and it took effect in June 2018.

The law's title, the Responsible Job Creation Act, refers to a provision that requires staffing agencies to demonstrate an effort to place temp workers into permanent positions if such positions become available.[19] It was the first in the nation to attempt to end "permatemping."

The new law also prohibits temp agencies and host employers from charging workers for criminal background checks, credit reports, and drug tests. It requires a temp agency to provide transportation from a jobsite if it was provided to the jobsite. Temp agencies must file an annual report to the Illinois Department of Labor with data on the race and gender of the temp workers they hire and must inform workers about the equipment, protective clothing, and training required to perform the job. The new law also mandates that workers be paid for a set minimum of hours, even if there's less work than anticipated. Workers can't be hired for a day's work and then be sent home after only an hour or two.

Why did Gallegos stick with the campaign to improve the temp industry?

"I got really angry at knowing and realizing that it didn't matter . . . that they would treat people as disposable," she said. "Change is difficult, but it's possible, even if it's just one person who speaks up."

Looking ahead, CWC wants to use the law to weed out the bad actors and elevate the good ones. The worker center and the Raise the Floor Alliance want the state to implement a "seal of approval" certification for staffing agencies administered through the Illinois Department of Labor. The certification would indicate that the staffing agency is complying with the new law. CWC and its allies envision a future in which companies would be required to use only staffing agencies that had been certified.

CWC's executive director, Tim Bell, told the *Chicago Sun-Times* that the responsible temp agencies support the proposal. "They see this as a game-changer. This gives the good agencies a chance to market themselves and get work."[20]

And that would be another win for Illinois's temp workers.

At New Labor in New Jersey, improving the staffing industry has always been on the worker center's to-do list. Co-founder Carmen Martino, a labor studies professor at Rutgers, noticed how the industry seemed to pop up overnight. On his commute, Martino "started to notice, driving in the very, very early mornings, lines of people that were waiting at temp agencies that had just basically sprung up overnight," he said.

The workers were at the Jersey part of a global web of trade spun out of distant lands across the sea and entering the United States through the Port Newark–Elizabeth Marine Terminal. From there, cargo was transported dozens of miles inland to distribution centers and warehouses in northern and central New

Jersey, where workers, hired by the day, the week, or the month, sorted, picked, bundled, and rerouted sneakers, rock salt, televisions, and furniture, all part of the billions of dollars of goods moving through the port.[21]

Martino and his colleague, George Gonos, mapped the area and found that all of the "industrial-sector temp agencies were located in, or within a couple of blocks of, residential neighborhoods with the highest concentrations (over 64 percent) of Latino residents."[22]

In their study, they noted that "New Brunswick, just 10–15 miles from the cluster of facilities at [New Jersey Turnpike] Exit 8A, and home to desirable pools of workers, is the epicenter of agency activity, the primary source of temp labor for the [warehouses and distribution centers]. That city's Latino neighborhoods have the highest concentration of temp agencies in the state—17 offices within a 1.4 mile radius."

They wrote, "It is 35–40 miles from the waterfront where low-wage agency temps, at the very bottom of the pyramid of the logistics industry, become a vital part of the global supply chain."

So curious were they about the nature of the work that they dispatched Lou Kimmel, now New Labor's executive director, and then a recent college graduate, to infiltrate the staffing agencies, getting temporary jobs in factories and warehouses. Like his fellow temps, Kimmel experienced many of the common problems—wage theft, lack of safety equipment and training, and being stranded at jobsites when the agency's van didn't show up at the end of the day.

New Labor's membership has always been dominated by temp workers, because many have jobs through the staffing industry. The center has helped members recover back wages, including a case that made headlines. They took on Olympus Management Services, Atlantis Personnel, and other related staffing firms to recoup $100,000 in unpaid temp worker wages.

New Labor was part of a statewide coalition that secured an

earned paid sick leave law in 2018. The worker center campaigned
to ensure that temp workers were covered by the law. New Labor's
efforts paid off. Now in New Jersey, even if temp workers go on
assignment to different companies, they accrue sick leave through
the agency that places them.

New Labor's effectiveness at organizing workers and their
members' success at winning campaigns for temp workers provide
motivation. As the worker center ticks off things on its to-do list,
it adds even more.

New Labor wants a law in New Jersey that builds on Massachusetts' Temporary Workers Right to Know Act and Illinois's
Responsible Job Creation Act. One demand is wage parity.

"Temp workers doing the same job as full-time employees
should get the same rate," said Kimmel. The way New Labor sees
it, if a company needs temp workers to resolve a pressing staffing
situation, it should cost a premium, viewed as value-added.

Another goal relates to a growing concern for worker centers
nationwide. What provisions can they put into place to make sure
the laws they lobbied so hard to pass are enforced? For temporary
workers, New Labor, in alliance with worker centers across the
state, is now looking at the idea of a wage bond.

Many temporary staffing agencies already post bonds—a form
of insurance to compensate their customers for property damage
or loss attributed to temp workers. New Labor envisions requiring
agencies to post a similar bond to cover workers' wages. All too
often, workers get ripped off when an agency abruptly shuts down,
leaving an empty office and no trace of the owners.

"So far there are only bonds on the property," Kimmel said.
"They should be investing in the workers as well."

19

ALL WORK, NO PAY

It was getting rowdy in the main hall at the Workers Defense Project (WDP) in Austin and volunteers were busy putting out more chairs. The *tejano* music was turned down as the weekly "Workers in Action" general assembly began.

Two men and a woman were presented with their membership cards. They took a pledge to fight and organize to attain justice for workers. The hall filled with applause and cheers of encouragement.

Maria Luisa Torres Espinosa stood up. Her bright smile was especially so that night. After three months of effort with the WDP, she was handed a check for the $165 she was owed by an Austin restaurant. She was a part-time cook and her boss refused to pay her for two weeks of work. The owner said he didn't have the money.

Espinosa came to WDP on the advice of a friend. The worker center helped her send a letter to the restaurant owner. Then WDP followed up with phone calls and face-to-face meetings. Finally, he relented and paid up.

She urged workers to never give up. "We can't let anyone rob us of our money," she said, speaking in Spanish.

A woman named Emerita was at the meeting to talk with WDP's workplace justice committee. Emerita was part of a cleaning crew working at one of Austin's newest housing developments. After the painting was done and carpet installed, Emerita and others would scrub floors and polish windows to make the homes attractive to potential buyers.

Emerita said she worked from seven in the morning until nine at night, and wasn't paid properly for her time. She was getting the kind of runaround that is common for victims of wage theft. Her boss said he hadn't been paid yet from the general contractor, but the general contractor said that wasn't true. Emerita wanted the WDP to help her recoup $1,100 in wages for eleven days of cleaning. She said she'd do whatever it took, for as long as it took, to recover the wages she had earned. Seeing how other workers had succeeded, Emerita felt optimistic.

What Emerita and Espinosa experienced is known as wage theft, a term popularized in the 1990s by the National Interfaith Committee on Worker Justice, later known as Interfaith Worker Justice (IWJ). It includes not getting paid at all, being shorted for the hours actually worked, being paid less than the minimum wage, not getting paid overtime, or having unauthorized deductions taken from wages.

Wage theft is a serious problem, affecting millions of workers each year. A 2017 analysis by the Economic Policy Institute (EPI) put the loss to workers at over $8 billion annually, and that was examining data from only the nation's ten most populous states. Extrapolating, the EPI estimated that the total loss to workers nationwide exceeds $15 billion.[1] But the situation is worse. The EPI analysis just estimated losses where underpayments caused workers to earn less than the minimum wage. It didn't consider, for example, losses from unpaid overtime or when less money was paid than promised, even if minimum wage requirements had been met.

At WDP, providing help with wage theft cases is a service the worker center offers to low-wage workers in the community. The center will write to or call the employer on the worker's behalf. It'll help the worker file a police report or a complaint with the Texas Workforce Commission. These steps will help the individual worker, but they don't tackle the larger problem of systemic wage and hour violations.

Ultimately worker centers want to build worker power for social and economic change. Campaigns to strengthen legal protections against wage theft have been top on the list for most worker centers. They do more than just help the individual victims—they strengthen the organization's expertise, build its membership, and, in the process, develop new worker leaders.

In business-friendly Texas, getting new statewide worker protection laws passed is challenging. Also, the Lone Star State's legislature only meets in the odd-numbered years and just for 140 days. Facing that reality, WDP focused its efforts on closing a loophole in an existing state law.

The loophole? An employer could avoid a "criminal theft of service" prosecution if he paid just a fraction of what was owed the worker. By paying their workers just a few bucks, employers figured out that local district attorneys would be unlikely to consider the lack of *full* payment a crime. If workers wanted to recoup all owed wages, they could file lawsuits in small claims courts.[2] The employers knew how unlikely that was.

WDP saw unscrupulous businesses using the loophole to game the system. The worker center pitched the idea of closing the loophole to a local lawmaker. Within five months of being introduced, it passed the state legislature with only one dissenting vote. Lawmakers seemed swayed by issues of fairness—for the workers themselves, but also for businesses undercut by dishonest employers. Governor Rick Perry signed the bill and it took effect in September 2011.

"Prosecutors and law enforcement officials all over Texas will be able to use this to send a strong message to employers who cheat their workers," said Emily Timm, who co-founded WDP in 2006.[3]

Worker centers elsewhere have engaged in different campaigns to address wage theft in their communities.

In Miami, an affiliate of IWJ co-founded the Florida Wage Theft Task Force in 2007. Foreign-born workers in the region's flower nurseries, construction sites, and fruit and vegetable farms were easy targets for wage theft and unlikely to file complaints. The task force organized workshops to educate workers about their rights, while legal aid groups were helping some recoup unpaid wages. Researchers with Florida International University who were task force members provided data and worker stories on the impact of wage theft on individuals and the local economy.[4] Shame also worked. The Florida Immigrant Coalition, American Friends Service Committee, South Florida IWJ, and other allies were not shy about demonstrating outside of the worst offending businesses. They'd hold signs that read, "Bosses, Don't Abuse Your Workers" and "Wage Theft Is a Crime."

The county commissioners of Miami-Dade County were persuaded when they read and heard about workers' experiences. Particularly disturbing were the examples involving laborers who hadn't been paid by subcontractors with county contracts. In February 2010, the commissioners passed the nation's first countywide wage theft law. It set up an administrative process and hearings to reconcile complaints of unpaid wages. A valid complaint could result in the employer being assessed triple damages and the cost of the hearing.

The precedent set in Miami-Dade provided momentum for the Florida Wage Theft Task Force to pursue similar ordinances in other counties. South Florida IWJ's Biblical references, such as "thou shall not steal," resonated with some lawmakers. Others were swayed by arguments that dishonest businesses had an unfair competitive advantage or that taxpayers would have to bear the burden when unpaid breadwinners needed to rely on county social services. Within five years, the task force pushed the counties of Alachua, Broward, Hillsborough, Osceola, and Pinellas to adopt "wage recovery" ordinances.

Even though the problem of wage theft is as pronounced in New

Jersey as anywhere else, replicating the county ordinances passed in Florida was not an approach available to New Jersey worker centers. In the Garden State, localities are prohibited from enacting laws that conflict with or preempt state laws. The state had an existing wage theft law, but it was too weak to make a difference.

A 2011 survey of day laborers in seven New Jersey cities found that more than half were paid less than the amount promised at least once during the past year.[5] A third of them said the amount owed was $100 to $500, perhaps part of a month's rent. Practically none filed complaints with the state's department of labor, for a resolution that may take more than a year.[6]

In New Brunswick, Catholic Charities' Unity Square and the New Labor worker center surveyed local neighborhoods to gauge the prevalence of the problem. They found that one in six households had experienced wage theft in the previous two years and only 15 percent of them were able to recover their wages.

"Often, you are not talking about very much money for an employer," Craig Garcia, an organizer with New Labor, told *NJ Spotlight*. But on the worker's end, "you are talking about being kicked out of your house or not being able to feed your family."[7]

Unity Square and New Labor worked with the New Brunswick City Council to draft an ordinance that would work around the state preemption. The idea was simple. If an employer is liable and has refused to pay owed wages, the business wouldn't be able to renew its city operating license.

Members of New Labor packed the city council chambers in December 2013 to show support for the proposed ordinance. They held up homemade signs: "Luchar para Prevenir el Robo de Salarios" (Fight to Prevent Wage Theft) and "Necesitamos una Ordenanza Contra el Robo de Salarios" (We Need a Wage Theft Ordinance).

The ordinance—the first of its kind in New Jersey—passed the five-member council unanimously.

The mayor, James Cahill, praised the measure. "Companies

that take part in such behavior have no place in New Brunswick and the city will not condone businesses that engage in this type of illegal activity."[8]

New Labor teamed up with New Jersey Working Families, Make the Road New Jersey, and the Immigrant Justice Alliance to pressure other localities to adopt similar license restrictions. By the end of 2016, Jersey City, Highland Park, East Orange, and Newark had measures on their books that were similar to New Brunswick's, with the city of Princeton adopting a narrower version in 2014.

Along the way, New Labor didn't give up its larger goal of a better wage theft law statewide. The bill's primary sponsor, Assemblywoman Annette Quijano, recognized the impact of unpaid wages on families in her district. Over the three legislative sessions the bill was considered, she often said, "No one should be withheld one penny of the wages to which they are legally entitled."[9]

In August 2019, New Labor's members celebrated the signing of the New Jersey Wage Theft Act, described as one of the most stringent in the nation. It was the culmination of years of campaigning by New Labor and allies pushing anti–wage theft bills in six municipalities in New Jersey.

Penalties include jail time for business owners and the ability of the state to withhold businesses licenses from employers or their successor companies. The state can also issue immediate cease-and-desist orders, shutting down violators' businesses on the spot.

However, the workers' movement for justice didn't end with that campaign victory.

"The fight doesn't stop here," New Labor wrote in an email announcing the news. "Together we got the bill passed; now help us enforce it."

20

THE FIGHT DOESN'T STOP HERE

Maria Colin felt conflicted. She knew she was being exploited by the family that hired her. She was caring for their children and doing the housework, but was only making $2 per hour. Maria thought she couldn't complain because she was grateful to have a job and a place to live. "I felt like they were doing me favor especially because I'm an immigrant and I don't speak English."

Six years later, Maria Colin came to learn about her workplace rights at the Graton Day Labor Center in California's wine country. She is now an influential voice in statewide and national campaigns for domestic workers.

Advocacy campaigns to make social change for low-wage and vulnerable workers are what distinguish worker centers from community-based direct service organizations. These worker centers may pursue campaigns against abusive employers or press for changes in city policies or state laws. The topic, strategy, tactics, and timeline depend on a multitude of factors, but they must be worker designed and worker led.

Across the nation, the result has been new laws involving wage theft, construction safety, temp worker protections, sick leave, and rest breaks for all kinds of workers from housekeepers to dairy hands. But how would these new laws be enforced?

At the Graton Day Labor Center, Maria Colin is a leader of the Alianza de Mujeres Activas y Solidarias. She meets with lawmakers in the state capitol on behalf of the California Domestic Workers Coalition. In 2019, she traveled to Washington, D.C., to speak in support of legislation ensuring that domestic workers receive fair wages and benefits, as well as safety and anti-discrimination protections.[1]

Many, if not most, domestic workers in situations like Maria's recognize they are being exploited. Likewise, garment workers in Los Angeles's "cut and sew" industry know they are being manipulated when they are paid a piece rate rather than at least the minimum wage. Day laborers repairing roofs understand the need for safety equipment, but often don't even have a hard hat.

Their circumstances are precarious. Asking to be paid legal wages, to get the required safety equipment, or to be free from sexual harassment may result in being fired. For those who are unauthorized to work in the United States, the threat of an immigration raid always looms. It's hard to fathom complaining to a boss when it's already difficult to make ends meet.

Worker centers help vulnerable workers see that change is possible. They educate workers about their labor rights, but beyond that, they provide proof that systemic change is possible through collective action. "The importance of political action cannot be overemphasized because it is in the course of political struggle that workers are able to learn that victories can be won," sociologists Edna Bonacich and Richard Appelbaum write. "The very act of participation is radicalizing because it undermines the oppressive belief that the employers are all-powerful and that change is impossible."[2]

Shifting the power dynamic is key to worker organizing and it happens through campaigns at worker centers. It took political action by farmworkers with the Coalition of Immokalee Workers to secure a penny a pound more in wages for the tomatoes they pick. In Austin, Texas, members of the Workers Defense Project secured a city ordinance mandating rest breaks for construction workers. In Morganton, North Carolina, a worker demonstration outside the Case Farms poultry plant was meant to shame the company for denying employees access to the bathroom.

Decisions about campaigns must come from those who are affected. It begins with a process of reflection, explained Martha Ojeda, senior national organizer with Interfaith Worker Justice.

"It is a process of thinking differently about how you are living in order to find a way to transform that reality. We work together to ask, 'Why is this happening?' And you guide them until they realize what is going on. Then they say, 'Enough, no way.' But they have to go through that process of reflection."

Ojeda understands why campaigns fail. She has seen well-meaning worker center boards and staff who decide they *need* to have a campaign. They identify a topic. They know allies in the community, such as faith leaders and local unions, who will endorse the campaign. They might even have some funders in mind.

"I've told them, 'You are trying to run the campaign from the desk. You're trying to run the campaign from the top, for all the allies, for all the external people, instead of from those who are affected," Ojeda said.

You can have "a beautiful campaign on paper," she added. "It's going to fail because you don't have those who will really be carrying it on to take ownership of it."

Imagine a group activity with two teams, Ojeda explained. One team has all the equipment. The referee loves them and lets them do whatever they want. The players on the other team don't have any shoes. They are blindfolded and their legs are tied to one another. The referee is against them.

"I do many exercises on power analysis," she said, describing the first stages of putting together a campaign. Workers need to do the exercises to get to the root of the problem. "They need to analyze what they really want to alter in the power relationship. Somebody is in power provoking what is happening. How can we change that labor relationship?

"The long-term goal might take two or three years. But in the meantime, how are you going to keep the people engaged and committed?" she asked. "So you need to have short-term goals. Those short-term goals are what they are going to need to do."

How many neighborhoods have you visited? How many are you going to visit in a month? How many on the city council are likely in favor? How many opposed? How many can come to the middle? What do you think of this? What about that?

"All these steps, all these questions," she said. "We are following the steps in order for them to be engaged. All of the plans need to come from the workers." So does the motivation. How does a worker center keep people involved when it might take several years to achieve a goal? And what happens if they don't ultimately achieve it?

Preparing for defeat is part of worker-led campaigns. "It is a process—*companiento*—you and I will work through the hard moments, through the hard times," Ojeda said. "Whatever happens for good or not, you are not alone. That is the process of *companiento*—together."

Planning effective campaigns that keep workers engaged for the long haul will include a lot of talk about the timeline. The plan, Ojeda explained, might be for three years, and "these are going to be the measures that we are going to accomplish to see if we are really advancing best."

That's why, Ojeda explained, campaigns need to list short-term goals that become the "wins" along the way. They are the accomplishments that will keep workers engaged for the long run.

Over this time period, are there more members? Are there new allies? Have fundraising goals been reached?

"And it's not just the number of this or the number of that, but qualitative," she said.

"Do we have leaders who are going to be inspiring the other ones? What is the reputation and credibility of the center's position in the community?"

In Houston, when Ojeda was an organizer with Fe y Justicia Worker Center, there were many workers seeking assistance for wage theft.

Ojeda was in neighborhoods, meeting with groups of workers in their homes. Each would share a story of how the employer didn't pay what was owed. Ojeda recounted the workers' conversations: "Today it is you, and then you, and then you. We can be doing this forever." Then Ojeda said she asked them: " 'What do we need to change? What do we need to do to alter that power relationship?' "

The answer—after lots of brainstorming—came from the workers themselves. "If I go and tell them 'you have to do this,' they're not going to do it," Ojeda said.

The "Down with Wage Theft" campaign in Houston powered up in February 2013. Members of Fe y Justicia Worker Center took ownership of the campaign. When the city council passed an anti–wage theft ordinance ten months later, in November, Houston became only the second major city in the southern United States to do so.

Hunter Ogletree, co-director of the Western North Carolina Workers' Center, explained, "It's important to decide in our planning how we will define a win and how we measure it. We make sure we celebrate all of our wins. We do it in a very culturally appropriate way, having cake, involving the whole family, maybe a barbecue outside where people can come and eat.

"You know, if you're not having fun—within a context of working on issues that are very depressing sometimes—people are going to burn out," he said. "But just because you have a victory doesn't mean you let off the pressure."

That's how campaigns work. "Working people suffer," said Adam Kader, director of Arise Chicago Worker Center, as he laid out the classic cycle of the struggle between the working class and the capital class. "Working people organize, and we figure out ways to put pressure on [government] so that it re-regulates practices around capital."

• • •

It might appear as though workers are leading when cities and
states pass shiny new laws protecting workers against wage theft,
lack of sick pay, unsafe working conditions, or shady practices by
temporary staffing agencies. There are the usual press conferences
with triumphant speeches by workers. Banners wave as workers
pose for the usual photographs in their matching T-shirts, their
fists raised in victory.

And then? Nothing. No enforcement. No punishment. No
consequences.

No wonder there's a drive for something more.

"You need to define what is *really* your goal," said Ojeda, who
has facilitated campaigns at worker centers around the country.
She recalled a meeting she attended with domestic workers in
Houston who were discussing their future campaign and getting
advice from domestic workers from New York. The Houston
workers were trying to decide whether to push for a Domestic Worker Bill of Rights, like the one passed in New York
in 2010.

"Sometimes [the goal you identify] it's not really the *right* goal.
That is what happened in New York. I think that NDWA made a
mistake," she said.

In New York, the National Domestic Workers Alliance
(NDWA) met a goal with a bill of rights—largely a symbolic measure, absent enforcement, one that did not seem to change the day-
to-day reality for housekeepers, nannies, and home care workers.
Ojeda explained, quoting the New York workers: "The women
said, 'We did not win nothing. For us, we won nothing.'"

It's a new refrain—not the part about winning nothing, but the
drive to safeguard what has been won.

"In the past, it was 'Let's pass new laws. Let's pass new laws.
Now we're done,'" said Shelly Ruzicka, Arise's communications
director. But, she said, the ineffectiveness of laws on paper to

guarantee labor protections "speaks to worker centers and why worker centers exist. If the laws were all followed, we might not exist.

"That's how a lot of us were first formed," she said, "helping the community on the most basic of laws—not being paid minimum wage, not being paid overtime, not being paid at all or for all hours of work, very basic health and safety, discrimination.

"So, it's kind of a new idea," she said. "It's great to pass laws, but if we don't enforce them, what's the point, because we know employers don't follow the law."

In Chicago, Arise, in alliance with other city worker centers, successfully lobbied the city to create the Office of Labor Standards to enforce the Chicago laws regarding minimum wage, ($14 per hour in July 2020), paid sick leave, and a predictable work schedule. The office, with a small staff of investigators, began operations in 2019.

Ruzicka said the inklings of the idea began shortly after Chicago passed a citywide minimum wage bill in 2013 and intensified after Arise and allies pushed the passage of paid sick leave in the Windy City. "I like to quote one of our members, Martina," Ruzicka said. "Right after we won, she said, 'This is so great that we won and we should celebrate, but we need to make sure that workers know their rights under this law and employers know their responsibilities.'"

Arise began by studying similar offices in Seattle, San Francisco, and New York, and settled on Seattle's version as the best fit for Chicago. Soon Arise's members visited aldermen, knocked on politicians' doors, testified at hearings, and spoke to journalists, all to build support.

"It's historic," Ruzicka said. "We remind ourselves that our organization, which means our worker members—low-wage immigrant workers—just requested and won from the city [an agreement] to create an entire new government office to protect them.

"This was not a top-down like the mayor said or an alderman saying, 'We should do this,'" she said. "This was workers saying, 'We're not always paid right or treated right and you, as a city government, it should be your responsibility to protect us. And we're demanding you create an office.' And we won it. We're really proud. It's a huge accomplishment."

The need for enforcement mechanisms is key—as coffee shop workers in upstate New York found to their chagrin.

In November 2009, Ana Ottoson, a cashier at Green Café in Ithaca, quit her job and turned to the Tompkins County Workers' Center, reporting that bussers and dishwashers at the café weren't getting paid, weren't receiving overtime, and weren't getting any days off. The center spearheaded an investigation by New York's Department of Labor, which uncovered similar violations in a coffee shop run by the same owner in New York City.

In September 2010, the state Department of Labor determined that the owner owed $623,000 for wage violations in Ithaca and $377,000 in New York. That was the good news. The bad news? Six months earlier, the owner had filed for bankruptcy and closed his businesses. The workers have never been paid.

The case exposed a major loophole in the law. A report by several advocacy groups found that over a ten-year period from 2003 to 2013, the New York State Department of Labor had been unable to collect $101 million dollars its investigators said businesses owed workers. Hardest hit? Low-wage workers, the kind who make up the membership of worker centers.[3]

Because of the Green Café incident, and others, the Tompkins County Workers' Center, other New York worker centers, and allies across the state have been pursuing state legislation that would allow liens to be attached to the assets of companies accused of wage violations. It would also permit workers to hold the ten largest shareholders of non–publicly traded corporations personally liable for unpaid wages.

Known as SWEAT (Securing Wages Earned Against Theft),

the measure passed both New York's Senate and Assembly, making it all the way to Governor Andrew Cuomo's desk for signing. But, on December 31, 2019, Cuomo vetoed the bill on what he said were technical grounds, disappointing advocates. Cuomo promised to put something similar in place in the future.

"Getting a result on this legislation will change lives, and is too important to risk its viability in the court system," Cuomo said in a memo dated January 1, 2020.

One method for enforcement is to tie compliance with wage laws to a business's ability to open its doors and turn on the lights.

That's what happened in New Brunswick, the New Jersey headquarters of New Labor. The city's wage theft law, passed in December 2013, linked enforcement to an annual renewal of an operating license. If there's a legal finding that wages are owed, employers must pay up or they'll forfeit their licenses.

In 2017, the law was put to the test when a New Brunswick sports bar, World of Beer, agreed to pay $57,500 to settle a case brought by six former employees accusing the company of wage and hour violations. The money was never paid; some of the owners left the business, and World of Beer opened under a new name, Hub City Brewhouse.

When Hub City Brewhouse's business license came up for renewal, the employees' lawyers petitioned the city to enforce the wage theft law and deny the business's license. The workers got their money.

"It was definitely effective," said New Labor executive director Lou Kimmel. "It's another tool and mechanism for people getting paid. In an ideal world, we wouldn't need this, because employers would pay their workers, but when they don't, this serves as a deterrent."

Sometimes the mere threat of enforcement can make a difference. That was the situation in upstate New York, where worker centers advocating on behalf of immigrant dairy hands urged local offices of the U.S. Occupational Safety and Health Administration (OSHA) to look into serious health and safety issues at the state's dairy farms.

Through surveys, the Worker Justice Center of New York and the Workers' Center of Central New York (WCCNY) had already learned about the use of dangerous chemicals; the possibility of injury from agitated cows, calves, and bulls, as well as the potential to drown in manure lagoons or to slip on freezing mounds of feed.

Some workers quit: one dairy hand suffered three serious injuries—pushed by a cow, a painful fall, and temporary blindness from the chloroform used to prevent fungus in the cows' hooves. The worker told Rebecca Fuentes, WCCNY's lead organizer, that he was leaving the farm. "He said, 'I'm quitting. My life is worth more than $7.25 an hour.'"

Researching farm conditions, Fuentes also learned about an OSHA initiative that allows local offices to focus on high-hazard industries. The agency's Local Emphasis Program (LEP) involves targeted outreach to employers with information and focused inspections. There was precedent. In 2011, OSHA's Wisconsin offices began an LEP on dairy farms.

In August 2013, advocates and dairy workers met with the New York regional OSHA director to request a similar LEP. He agreed, at first. "We were so happy that the workers' stories had impact," Fuentes said. "This was going to be a game changer.

"But then we realized we had awakened the beast," she said. "We started to see the influence of the New York Farm Bureau and Cornell University Cooperative Extension. We realized that the industry was becoming very active."

Members of Congress, hounded by the state's powerful dairy lobby, signed a letter asking OSHA to delay the program's start. Workers responded with an eleven-day, twenty-three-stop media blitz to raise awareness, broaden public support, and cultivate new partnerships.

Tragically, events helped their efforts. On March 20, 2014, the workers had scheduled a meeting with U.S. Rep. Daniel Maffei, a Democrat from Syracuse.

"The day we went to pick up a worker for the meeting, there was a fatality at that farm," Fuentes said. "You could see the police. An American worker who was a mechanic got crushed by a machine. Two workers came from that farm, and what a powerful message they had to bring with them."

Even without the LEP, the workers were already making progress. OSHA began to include both farmers and workers in its outreach calls about health and safety issues on dairy farms. "Part of fighting back was demanding that OSHA—just like they have to talk to the industry—they have to talk to the workers," Fuentes said.

Finally, in 2015, OSHA announced the dairy LEP.

"Workers started getting some training and some protective equipment. The workers got to see that change," Fuentes said.

"The biggest impact was that just the threat and the potential for [farms] being inspected was enough [to push them into] providing equipment, providing training, and fixing hazards," Fuentes said.

"That," she said, "is the power of enforcement."

Rebecca Fuentes, former lead organizer, Workers' Center
of Central New York, Syracuse. *I. George Bilyk*

THE POWER AWAKENED

The river of workers in New Labor's trademark orange T-shirts coursed through New Brunswick's faded inner-city Latino neighborhood, part of the Worker Memorial Day March and Rally sponsored each April by the worker center.

That was 2019, when solidarity in New Jersey meant shoulder-to-shoulder, side-by-side, chanting, "Ni una muerta mas" (Not one more death).

In April 2020—because of the COVID-19 pandemic—that somber parade through the streets of New Brunswick was replaced by livestream and grainy video footage, experienced in kitchens and living rooms. No side-by-side, no shoulder-to-shoulder, just faces visible across the lonely internet.

But with eyes closed, it almost sounded like the event from previous years: Alternating verses of *Solidarity Forever* in Spanish and English. The rallying cry "Ni una muerta mas" rang with particularly poignant fervor, the sadly similar stories of a brother, wife, or son dying on the job, and as usual, the solemn reading of names of workers who went to work and never came home.

No one could hug or shake hands, but warmth came through as participants wrote comments in chat boxes that popped up next to the videos.

"Hola compañeros, saludos y abrazos para todos ustedes," Yolanda Hernandez wrote. "Hello comrades, greetings and hugs to all of you."

"Todo a la lucha al respecto Derechos y Dignidad!!!, somos

trabajadores esenciales para la Labor. . . . Todo Somos NEW LA-BOR!!!," she continued, still typing in the chat box. "All for the struggle for respect, rights and dignity. We are essential workers for Labor. We are New Labor."

Rising Newark politician Victor Monterrosa Jr., always the master of ceremonies, rose to his livestreaming task, a true natural communicator in English and Spanish, online and off.

"Tenemos poder; we have power," he said, leading the group in applause, oddly solitary, as the audience was muted. What's the sound of one man clapping?

Monterrosa said people hope life will return to normal, but "we cannot return to normal," he said. If so, it will be a "return to all the same problems we had. We cannot go back to that."

If the new normal looks like old normal, then the members of New Labor and other worker centers around the nation will still be fighting to get paid fair wages, or any wages, for their work. There will still be the same sad stories like the one Janet Caicedo told, speaking online after Monterrosa.

Her brother, temp worker Edilberto Caicedo, a forklift operator, died when his skull was crushed on the job on August 22, 2019. When his family went through his papers later, they saw from his paystubs that he had been improperly paid. The old normal: wage theft; dying at work.

Will normal mean that workers still struggle with isolation, harassment, and disrespect, unable to get sick pay, overtime, or a reasonable schedule?

No one needs that "normal," Monterrosa said. "We are going to get ourselves out of this crisis and improve conditions for our workers on the job."

Meanwhile, in many supermarkets in early spring 2020, the new normal looked like this: Meat cases were nearly empty. No more boneless breast of chicken on sale. A few lonely curls of sausage shared shelf space with a single package of beef cubes, brown at the edges, somehow overlooked. Animals piled up at the slaughterhouses. At food processing plants, shuttered one by one in March, April, and May 2020 in response to outbreaks of COVID-19 among workers, there was no one to turn steers into steaks.

That's how poor working conditions, usually hidden behind factory walls, looked to the rest of America, accustomed to cruising through supermarkets, carts piled high with hamburger, eggs, and milk.

It was the same in nursing homes. Food that had been mediocre at best was being served in plastic containers to seniors sitting alone in their rooms. Who was there to care for lonely grandmothers and elderly parents?

The same question applied to suburban cul-de-sacs, where harried young professionals in home offices tried to juggle meetings, reports, and workday responsibilities with wiping up spills and building forts out of blankets in the living room. Where were the nannies and the housekeepers? What about the gardeners? The lawns needed haircuts and so did the homeowners inside.

The question that most of us in America will have to answer going forward is whether we are willing, or even able, to pay the actual price, the just price, for the goods and services we use. We've accepted our easy access—from T-bone steaks to $10 T-shirts—as our prerogative as long as we don't think too hard or examine what we're doing too closely. What will the real price be to cover fair wages and safe conditions for home care workers, meatpackers, sewing machine operators, and day laborers?

It's a question that workers have long asked, but the answers haven't been forthcoming. Doesn't everyone deserve sick pay? Doesn't everyone deserve to be paid adequately for their work? Shouldn't every workplace be safe—COVID-19 or not?

In industry after industry, from real estate and office space, from farms to restaurants, from amusement parks to warehouses,

the COVID-19 pandemic has sharpened the nation's focus on
equity, even as the people who change bedpans, deliver packages,
and slaughter chickens struggle to stay alive—and get paid.

What is the true price? How society responds will play out over
time.

But in the meantime, worker centers weren't waiting—not
when unemployment for Latinos jumped from 4.4 percent to
18.9 percent between February and April 2020 and the April
rate for Blacks was 16.7 percent. And not when worker centers,
as trusted community organizations, found themselves in the best
position to help.

Unlike traditional labor unions, sometimes hamstrung by bureaucracies and regulations, worker centers are more flexible and
in more immediate touch with their members. They often live in
the same community. They speak the same language, whether it's
Spanish, Tagalog, Mam, or Somali.

Worker centers met some immediate needs by distributing
groceries to those who lost their jobs or had their work hours significantly reduced. The Western North Carolina Workers' Center (WNCWC) created a rapid response fund to help immigrant
workers who did not qualify for the financial assistance passed
by Congress. They made a direct appeal to supporters to raise
$50,000. "In a time where everything is unclear the only thing we
can rely on is collective support," the center wrote on its website.

But WNCWC wasn't turning into a soup kitchen. The pandemic was not going to sidetrack what worker centers have emphasized all along—not charity, but building worker power for
lasting change.

Cultivating leadership and the power of workers to demand
change is the heart and soul of the worker center movement.
It was on full display during the 2020 coronavirus pandemic.
Members of the Pilipino Workers Center met in a virtual town
hall with members of Congress to demand safety protections for
home care workers, including its members from the Philippines.

A meatpacking worker with the Rural Community Workers Alliance in Green City, Missouri, filed a federal lawsuit to compel Smithfield Foods to institute physical distancing in its plants. And after the governor of Florida ignored multiple requests for COVID-19 testing in farmworker communities, he succumbed to pressure from the Coalition of Immokalee Workers, which amassed forty thousand signatures on a petition.

In Morganton, North Carolina, workers at the Case Farms poultry processing plant continued to work. The federal government designated food production a critical infrastructure industry. The relentless speed of the assembly line continued. Just like the company's unwillingness to allow bathroom breaks, it wasn't providing face masks or gloves. Workers were still standing shoulder to shoulder as they cut up chicken parts and packaged them.

Then the first worker tested positive for COVID-19. "It was only a matter of time," said Magaly Urdiales, the co-director of WNCWC.

A member of the center who works at the plant saw a disaster waiting to happen—the virus taking hold in the plant and then spreading to everyone's family. She filed a safety complaint with the North Carolina Department of Labor's Division of Occupational Safety and Health. It was an example of leadership that Urdiales has nurtured for ten years at the center.

"Leadership means a worker taking ownership of their space, of their life, and having the tools they need to do that," she said. "It's a beautiful thing when we do things to make our community better."

In Minnesota, COVID-19 made it more important than ever for the Greater Minnesota Worker Center (GMWC) to mobilize poultry workers and elevate the problem of unsafe conditions in the local processing plants. More than one hundred employees walked off the job on April 27, 2020, at the Pilgrim's Pride facility in Cold Springs. The worker center held a virtual press conference to accompany the walkout. Mohamed Goni, the staff organizer, translated the testimonials of the Somali-speaking workers.

"In the next two weeks, if something isn't done, it will be out of hand and we'll be in a very, very bad situation," he said.[1] The workers' "pressure and persuasion" tactics, Goni said, would not let up.

Fourteen days later, when the Minnesota Department of Health reported 194 cases among employees at the Cold Springs, Minnesota, plant—more than double the number from just a few days earlier—GMWC and the interfaith group, Asamblea de Derechos Civiles, organized a "car vigil" demonstration that circled the Pilgrim's Pride plant.

One vehicle had a bullhorn propped out the window, ready to lead the caravan in chants when it paused. Cars were decorated with homemade signs with familiar slogans: "Keep me safe at work" and "Safety over profits." The timely message displayed on some car windows spoke to the COVID-19 crisis: "Essential, not disposable."

Orchestrating a car protest was a new way to telegraph the energy that comes from a public display of solidarity. But worker centers have also had to innovate to keep members connected to each other.

The need to physical distance meant no weekly in-person gatherings or face-to-face training workshops. Staffers settled into rounds of conference calls and online meetings, but "organizers say it's really hard to organize over the phone," said Arise Chicago's communication director, Shelly Ruzicka. "It's hard when you can't get a group of people in a room and drum up that energy. So much of organizing is providing moral support and giving them a hug. That's all missing now."

But those obstacles didn't stop Arise Chicago members from assisting workers from a medical supply factory with their demonstration. The workers outside of LSL Healthcare on May Day 2020 wore face masks, they stood six feet apart, and they handed their boss a letter demanding safety protections from the coronavirus.

COVID-19 has demonstrated that worker centers are nimble. Worker centers maximize the unforeseen. They remain strategic and intentional in all they do.

Worker centers have succeeded in battles against powerful foes, like the dairy industry, poultry companies, staffing agencies, and the ever-present shadow of racism. It's not only about a one-time victory—the passage of a new law, the change of a policy, the payment of wages past due.

What matters is that America—pushed, pulled, and pummeled by workers strengthened through solidarity—never returns to a new normal marked by exploitation and oppression. Everyone must pay the price of change.

There is a message of hope. As mighty and strong as employers are, aided and abetted by an economic system that favors the already-wealthy, labor activism is not a quaint notion from days gone by. Instead, it's growing, as workers in some of the most precarious employment situations are embracing strength in numbers, finding their voices, challenging those with power, and claiming their rights to fair wages, safe jobs, and decent work.

ACKNOWLEDGMENTS

The highlight of our research was spending time with the men and women from Arise Chicago, Centro de Derechos Laborales, Fe y Justicia Worker Center, Graton Day Labor Center, Greater Minnesota Worker Center, Latino Union of Chicago, New Labor, MassCOSH, Street Level Health Project, Tompkins County Workers' Center, and Workers' Center of Central New York. We are grateful to each of the people we met, for the generosity of their time, and the expertise they shared with us. This book would not have been possible had they not welcomed us through their doors. Their courage, ingenuity, and persistence inspired us, and we are deeply grateful for that inspiration. We will remember them forever. We thank everyone we interviewed, including:

Fatuma Abib
Kathy Ahoy
Ahmed Ali
Bethany Boggess Alcauter
Soledad Araque
Vanessa Bain
Myrla Baldonado
Milagros Barreto
Tim Bell
Debbie Berkowitz
Linda Burnham
Hortensia Bustos

Janet Caicedo
Greg Casar
Maria Colin
Maria Luisa Torres Espinosa
Jorge Estrada
Carly Fox
Rebecca Fuentes
Gabriela Galicia
Marcela Gallegos
Brenda de la Garza
José Granados
Gustavo Granillo

Marcy Goldstein-Gelb
Mohamed Goni
Crispin Hernandez
Yolanda Hernandez
Ania Jakubek
Adam Kader
Lou Kimmel
Magaly Licolli
Lolita Lledo
Alyssa Longobardi
Deysi Lopez
Isabel Lopez
Marsha Love
Christy Lubin
Consuelo Martínez
Carmen Martino
Francisco Matias
Jonas Mendoza
Pete Meyers
Nora Morales
Mirella Nava
Arturo Nieto
Hunter Ogletree
Mitzi Ordoñez
Maegan Ortiz
Aadhithi Padmanabhan

Hugo Perez
Laura Perez-Boston
Mario Pina
Nancy Plankey-Videla
Magdalena Pulla
Gretchen Purser
Lucy Quintanar
Analía Rodríguez
Diana Ramirez
Maria Rios
Shelly Ruzicka
Edgar Salazar
Erika Sanchez
Mirna Santizo
Mario Solano
Jodi Sugerman-Brozan
Emily Timm
Magaly Urdiales
Al Vega
Mariana Viturro
Hadio Wais
Joe Zanoni
Alejandro Zuniga
Nancy Zuniga
Magdalena Zylinska

Our writing was informed by other organizations that are advancing the worker center movement, including Casa Latina, CASA de Maryland, Chicago Workers' Collaborative, Coalition of Immokalee Workers, Food Chain Workers Alliance, Garment Worker Center, Gig Workers Collective, Immigrant Solidarity DuPage, Instituto de Educación Popular del Sur de California, National Council for Occupational Safety and Health and its network, National Day Laborer Organizing Network, National Domestic Workers Alliance, New Orleans Workers' Center for Racial Justice, Pilipino Workers Center, Restaurant Opportunities Center, The Workplace Project, Venceremos, Voces de la Frontera, Warehouse Workers United, Western North Carolina Workers' Center, Worker Justice Center of New York, Workers Defense Project, and the Workers' Justice Project in Brooklyn, New York.

We give a big thanks to Kim Krisberg, who wrote terrific stories about worker centers for *The Pump Handle* blog, where she was a contributor from 2011 to 2018. Her reporting about Fuerza del Valle in Texas's Rio Grande Valley, the Workers Defense Project in Austin, and other worker centers sparked the idea for this book. We are happy and grateful to include her work in *On the Job*.

Our book would not have been possible without the support of the Public Welfare Foundation. Our sincere appreciation goes to Bob Shull who had the vision for and directed the foundation's Workers' Rights program. Bob recognized the movement's success at building worker power and improving the well-being of low-wage workers. He saw these accomplishments before many in the foundation world and encouraged other funders to support the movement. Bob also recognized the value of a book to document this moment in time for worker centers.

We are grateful to Bob Shull for introducing us to Marc Favreau at The New Press. Beginning with our very first conversation, Marc gave us confidence that we could take on this project. He conveyed that we not only had the skills needed to write a book, but there was an audience for the stories we wanted to tell. Most importantly, he, like Bob, understood the importance of the worker center movement, not only for its members, but for all workers. We appreciate the support of Emily Albarillo, our wonderful production editor; Liana Krissoff, our amazing copy editor; and all of those behind the scenes at The New Press who made the publication process a breeze.

Finally, we thank Jason Cato and Lourdes Ontiveros for giving us permission to use his photograph and her powerful image on the book jacket.

I offer sincere thanks to all of the wonderful colleagues I've worked with over the years who shared their expertise, expanded my view of the world, and inspired me with their commitment to make the world a more healthy and just place. They include the people I worked with at the U.S. Department of Labor, faculty in the Department of Environmental and Occupational Health at the George Washington University, as well as the many social justice advocates whom I know through the American Public Health Association and the COSH Network. I am grateful for the time spent in work and conversation with all of them, especially Liz Borkowski, Peter Dooley, Andrea Hricko, Davitt McAteer, David Michaels, Mary Miller, Martha Ojeda, Tom O'Connor, Tony Oppegard, and Linda Reinstein. Thanks also to Howard Berkes, Jim Morris, and Ken Ward Jr. for their years of excellent reporting about workers and the lives lost because of employer indifference.

Finally, I am tremendously grateful to my co-author, Jane M. Von Bergen. She is a superb writer and because she relishes meeting new people and their places, Jane is a wonderful storyteller. Thanks to her, our pages are filled with the spirit and personality of worker centers. Jane was an extraordinary partner in this book-writing adventure. I never imagined that this endeavor could be a delight, but Jane made it so.

This book is dedicated to my wonderfully supportive husband, Jim Steenhagen, my parents Theresa and Roger Monforton, my siblings Lou, Tony, Roger, Dave, and Denise, and also to Russ who made me strong.

Celeste Monforton

My first acknowledgment goes to my co-author, Celeste Monforton. Her genuine compassion for workers, her absolute belief in their right to safe workplaces, and her valuable expertise in public and occupational health set us on the straight path from the start. Always ready with an encouraging word at the right time, Celeste's bright optimistic spirit made her a joy as a collaborator. Thank you, Celeste.

Tireless worker safety advocate Barbara Rahke, who formerly led both the National Council for Occupational Safety and Health and the Philadelphia Project on Occupational Safety and Health, deserves a big thank-you for introducing me to Celeste. I would not have met Barbara had I not had the privilege of covering labor for the *Philadelphia Inquirer*, one of America's great newspapers. I deeply appreciate my journalism colleagues and their feisty, frank, and fearless attitudes. As a journalist, I'm also grateful to the many people whose stories I told—each had a lesson for me and all of them, particularly workers, contributed to my understanding of the world.

I'm thankful beyond measure for my husband, I. George Bilyk, who, exhibiting remarkable love and patience, took most of the photographs in the book. Our sons, Michael and Joseph "Joey" Bilyk, along with my sister, Martha L. Dahan, mean the world to me, as does my beloved husband. This book is dedicated to the memory of my parents, Frederick J. and Lorraine M. Von Bergen. I thank them, and God, with all my heart.

Jane M. Von Bergen

NOTES

Chapter 1

1. We credit Kim Krisberg for her interviews with Joann Figueroa and Mirella Nava that were originally reported for *The Pump Handle* blog in "Worker Center Success: Houston Workers Organize for Safer Conditions at Insulation Plant," Oct. 23, 2015.

2. U.S. Occupational Safety and Health Administration, "Pipe Insulator and Staffing Agency Cited for Exposing Workers to Amputation," News Release, Aug. 17, 2015.

3. Janice Fine, *Worker Centers: Organizing Communities at the Edge of the Dream* (Ithaca, NY: Cornell University Press, 2006).

4. U.S. Bureau of Labor Statistics, "Census of Fatal Occupational Injuries Summary, 2018," News Release, Dec. 17, 2019; U.S. Bureau of Labor Statistics, "Survey of Occupational Injuries and Illnesses, Table 2, Number of Nonfatal Occupational Injuries and Illnesses by Industry and Case Type, 2018," News Release, Nov. 7, 2019.

5. North Carolina Department of Health and Human Services, Division of Public Health, *North Carolina Occupational Health Trends, 2000–2013* (Raleigh: NC Department of Health and Human Services, 2016), 5.

6. Jeanne M. Sears, Stephen M. Bowman, and Sheilah Hogg-Johnson, "Disparities in Occupational Injury Hospitalization Rates in Five States (2003–2009)," *American Journal of Industrial Medicine* 58, no. 5 (May 2015): 528–40.

7. Andrea L. Steege et al., "Examining Occupational Health and Safety Disparities Using National Data: A Cause for Continuing Concern," *American Journal of Industrial Medicine* 57, no. 5 (May 2014): 527–38.

Chapter 2

1. Michael King, "The View from Rio 21," *Austin Chronicle*, Dec. 25, 2009.

2. Workers Defense Project and the Division of Diversity and Community Engagement at the University of Texas, *Building Austin, Building Injustice: Working*

Conditions in Austin's Construction Industry (Austin, TX: Workers Defense Project, 2009).

3. Nora Ankrum, "Fighting for Justicia: Workers Defense Project Celebrates 10 Years on the Front Lines of Texas Labor," *Austin Chronicle*, Sept. 21, 2012.

4. We thank Kim Krisberg for her reporting about the Workers Defense Project and interviews with Bethany Boggess Alcauter, Greg Casar, and Diana Ramirez for *The Pump Handle* blog in "Austin Project Successfully Integrating Workers' Rights into Larger Sustainability Goals," June 18, 2012; "A Different Kind of Texas-Style Justice: Two Nights at Austin's Workers Defense Project," Aug. 31, 2012; and "In the Fight for a Rest Break, Dallas Construction Workers Find Their Voice," May 23, 2016.

5. Ankrum, "Fighting for Justicia."

6. King, "The View."

7. Ibid.

8. Workers Defense Project, *Building Austin*, 27.

9. Marty Toohey, "Construction Workers Must Get Rest Breaks, City Council Says," *Austin-American Statesman*, July 30, 2010.

10. The City of Austin adopted in 2012 its thirty-year comprehensive master plan, called "Imagine Austin." Its aim is for the city to be "a beacon of sustainability, social equity, and economic opportunity."

11. Workers Defense Project and the Center for Sustainable Development at the University of Texas, *Green Jobs for Downtown Austin: Exploring the Consumer Market for Sustainable Buildings* (Austin, TX: Workers Defense Project, 2013), 15.

12. Ibid., 19.

13. City of Austin, Texas: Ordinance No. 2017-0302-009.

14. Brenda de la Garza, City of Austin, Texas, phone interview with author, Aug. 14, 2019.

15. Workers Defense Project and the Division of Diversity and Community Engagement at the University of Texas, *Build a Better Texas: Construction Working Conditions in the Lone Star State* (Austin, TX: Workers Defense Project, 2013).

16. Workers Defense Project and the Division of Diversity and Community Engagement at the University of Texas, *Build a Better Nation: A Case for Comprehensive Immigration Reform* (Austin, TX: Workers Defense Project, 2013).

17. Steven Greenhouse, "The Workers Defense Project, a Union in Spirit," *New York Times*, Aug. 10, 2013.

18. The Workers Defense Project opened offices in Dallas in 2012 and in Houston in 2017.

Chapter 3

1. "Labor Enforcement Task Force," Department of Industrial Relations, State of California, accessed May 28, 2020, https://www.dir.ca.gov/letf/letf.html.

Chapter 6

1. Leslie C. Gates et al., "Sizing Up Worker Center Income (2008–2014): Study of Revenue Size, Stability, and Streams," in *No One Size Fits All: Worker Organization, Policy, and Movement in a New Economic Age*, ed. Janice Fine et al. (Champaign, IL: Labor and Employment Relations Association, 2018), 42.

Chapter 7

1. U.S. Chamber of Commerce, *Worker Centers: Union Front Groups and the Law* (Washington, D.C., 2018).

2. "Full-Page Ad in the Wall Street Journal Unmasks Big Labor's Latest Scheme," *Labor Pains* (blog), Center for Union Facts, July 25, 2013, https://labor pains.org/2013/07/25/full-page-ad-in-the-wall-street-journal-unmasks-big-labors -latest-scheme.

Chapter 8

1. "Gimme! Coffee Baristas Unanimously Ratify First Union Contract," Tompkins County Workers' Center, Feb. 7, 2018, https://www.tcworkerscenter .org/2018/02/gimme-coffee-baristas-unanimously-ratify-first-union-contract.

2. "Joint Board Welcomes Its Newest Local," *Reflections* 33, no. 138 (Fall 2015): 5.

3. National Center for Law and Economic Justice, the Legal Aid Society, and Urban Justice Center, *Empty Judgments: The Wage Collection Crisis in New York* (New York, 2015).

Chapter 9

1. "Building News You Can Use: Local Law 196, Safety Training Requirements," New York City Department of Buildings, https://www1.nyc.gov/assets /buildings/pdf/LL196_OnePager.pdf.

Chapter 10

1. Stephen E. Philion, "Distinguished Sociologist Award Speech" (plenary speech, Sociologists of Minnesota Conference, St. Cloud State University, St. Cloud, MN, Sept. 30, 2016).

2. Joseph A. McCartin, "Building the Interfaith Worker Justice Movement: Kim Bobo's Story," *Labor: Studies in Working-Class History of the Americas* 6, no. 1 (2009): 91.

3. Ibid., 105.

4. Kim Bobo served as the executive director of Interfaith Worker Justice until 2015. As of June 2020, she was the executive director of the Virginia Interfaith Center for Public Policy.

5. McCartin, "Building the Interfaith Worker," 101.

6. Kim Bobo, *Wage Theft in America: Why Millions of Working Americans Are Not Getting Paid and What We Can Do About It* (New York: The New Press, 2009), 270–76; McCartin, 97.

7. As of June 2020, Jose Oliva was campaign director of the HEAL Food Alliance.

8. Janice Fine has collaborated with and conducted research about worker centers since the 1990s. She has written extensively on labor organizing and new forms of unionism, including two books cited in these notes.

9. Philion, "Distinguished Sociologist."

10. Ibid.

11. Ibid.

12. Benjamin Hardy, "Study Slams Arkansas Poultry Processing Plants for Low Wages, Lack of Sick Leave," *Arkansas Times*, Feb. 9, 2016.

13. The Northwest Arkansas Workers' Justice Center was dissolved in 2019. Magaly Licolli, its former executive director, founded Venceremos in October 2019, a new worker justice organization located in Springdale, Arkansas.

14. Northwest Arkansas Workers' Justice Center, *Wages and Working Conditions in Arkansas Poultry Plants* (Springdale, AR: 2016).

15. "USA's 2020 Top Broiler Companies," *WATT Poultry USA* 21, no. 5 (Mar. 2020): 36.

16. Dillon Thomas, "Survey of Poultry Workers Claims to Expose Bad Working Environment," first broadcast Feb. 6, 2016, by KFSM-5 News (Fort Smith, AR).

17. Annette Bernhardt et al., *Broken Laws, Unprotected Workers: Violations of Employment and Labor Laws in America's Cities* (Chicago: University of Illinois,

Center for Urban Economic Development; National Employment Law Project; and University of California, Institute for Research on Labor and Employment, 2009).

18. Carly Fox et al., *Milked: Immigrant Dairy Farmworkers in New York State* (Syracuse, NY: Workers' Center of Central New York, 2017).

19. Garment Worker Center, UCLA Labor Center, and UCLA Labor Occupational Safety and Health, *Dirty Threads, Dangerous Factories: Health and Safety in Los Angeles' Fashion Industry* (Los Angeles: 2016).

20. Linda Burnham, Lisa Moore, and Emilee Ohia, *Living in the Shadows: Latina Domestic Workers in the Texas-Mexico Border Region* (New York: National Domestic Workers Alliance, 2018).

Chapter 11

1. Anna Haecherl, "Poultry Workers Rally for Workplace Safety, Better Conditions," *St. Cloud Times* (MN), Apr. 25, 2019.

Chapter 12

1. We credit Kim Krisberg for her reporting about domestic workers and interviews with Marsha Love, Mitzi Ordoñez, Laura Perez-Boston, Lucy Quintanar, and Magdalena Zylinska for *The Pump Handle* blog in "'Statistics Can't Tell Stories': Houston Domestic Workers Release Personal Anthology," May 6, 2014; and "Chicago Organizers Take on Domestic Worker Health and Safety," May 26, 2015.

2. As of June 2020, Laura Perez-Boston was with the Workers Defense Project.

3. As of June 2020, Mitzi Ordoñez was with the Texas Organizing Project.

4. As of February 2020, Myrla Baldonado was with the Pilipino Worker Center in Los Angeles.

Chapter 13

1. AFL-CIO, *Death on the Job: The Toll of Neglect* (Washington, D.C.: AFL-CIO, 2019).

2. "Funder Q&A with Robert Shull of the Public Welfare Foundation," Children, Youth & Family Funders Roundtable, June 11, 2018, https://fundersroundtable.org/2018/06/11/funder-qa-with-robert-shull-of-the-public-welfare-foundation.

Chapter 14

1. Thomas Maloney, Libby Eiholzer, and Brooke Ryan, *Survey of Hispanic Dairy Workers in New York State, 2016* (Ithaca, NY: College of Agriculture and Life Sciences, Cornell University, 2016), 4.

2. Based on data from the U.S. Bureau of Labor Statistics Census of Fatal Occupational Injuries, as reported annually for the years 2008 through 2018 in "Table 1: Fatal Occupational Injuries by Industry and Event or Exposure."

3. Data from the Bureau of Occupational Health and Injury Prevention, New York State Department of Health provided to Margaret Gray, Adelphi University, Feb. 29, 2016.

4. Rebecca Fuentes left the Workers' Center of Central New York in December 2019. As of June 2020, Fuentes was serving as a volunteer to assist worker groups, particularly a group maintaining a home in Syracuse for displaced farmworkers.

5. Donna A. Lupardo, New York State Assembly, "State Legislature Celebrates Dairy Day," News Release, June 5, 2019.

6. As of August 2020, Aadhithi Padmanabhan was a staff attorney with the New York Legal Aid Society.

7. Clara McMichael, "Farmworkers Struggle to Unionize in New York, Crispin Hernandez May Change That," *Documented*, Aug. 17, 2018.

8. Northeast Diary Foods Association, Inc., "June 5 is Dairy Day at the New York State Capitol," News Release, June 3, 2019.

9. Office of the New York State Comptroller, *Agriculture in New York State*, Sept. 2018, https://www.osc.state.ny.us/reports/economic/agriculture-report -2018.pdf.

10. New York State, Department of Agriculture and Markets, Division of Milk Control and Dairy Services, "Dairy Statistics, 2009, Annual Summary"; and U.S. Department of Agriculture, National Agricultural Statistics Service, "Milk Production," News Release, Dec. 18, 2007.

11. *Hernandez v. State*, 173 A.D.3d 105, 99 N.Y.S.3d 795 (N.Y. App. Div. 2019).

12. New York Farm Bureau, "Statement on Judicial Ruling in *Hernandez v. State of New York*," News Release, May 25, 2019.

Chapter 15

1. U.S. Government Accountability Office, *Workplace Safety and Health: Better Outreach, Collaboration, and Information Needed to Help Protect Workers at*

Meat and Poultry Plants (Washington, D.C.: Government Accountability Office, 2017).

2. Noelle Bellow, "Activists Protest for Sanderson Farms Workers Claiming Inhumane Working Conditions at Bryan Plant," first broadcast Oct. 1, 2018, by KBTX-TV (Bryan, TX).

3. In January 2020, OSHA and Sanderson Farms reached a formal settlement that resulted in the two serious violations being deleted and no monetary penalty assessed.

Chapter 16

1. President Donald J. Trump (@realDonaldTrump), "Next week ICE will begin process of removing the millions of illegal aliens . . . they will be removed as fast as they come in," Twitter, June 17, 2019.

Chapter 17

1. Monica Castillo, "Making Their Work 'Visible': Oscar-Nominated 'Roma' Spurs Domestic Workers to Activism," NBC News, Feb. 22, 2019.

2. Ai-jen Poo, "A Twenty-First Century Organizing Model: Lessons from New York Domestic Workers Bill of Rights Campaign," *New Labor Forum* 20, no. 1 (2011): 53.

3. Cara Buckley and Annie Correal, "Domestic Workers Organize to End an 'Atmosphere of Violence' on the Job," *New York Times*, June 9, 2008.

4. Steven Greenhouse, "New Protections for Nannies Are Approved by Council," *New York Times*, May 15, 2003.

5. Ai-jen Poo et al., "National Domestic Workers Alliance," in *The United States Social Forum: Perspectives of a Movement*, ed. Marina Karides et al. (Chicago: Changemaker Publications, 2010), 155–58.

6. Ibid., 156.

7. Poo, "A Twenty-First Century," 55.

8. Nicholas Confesore and Anemona Hartocollis, "Albany Approves No-Fault Divorce and Domestic Workers' Rights," *New York Times*, July 2, 2010.

9. Linda Burnham and Nik Theodore, *Home Economics: The Invisible and Unregulated World of Domestic Work* (New York: National Domestic Workers Alliance, 2012).

10. We credit Kim Krisberg for her reporting about domestic workers and interviews with Linda Burnham, Laura Perez-Boston, and Mariana Viturro for *The*

Pump Handle blog in "First-of-Its-Kind Survey Compiles the Experience of Domestic Workers," Dec. 7, 2012.

11. Women's Collective of La Raza Centro Legal, Mujeres Unidas y Activas, and DataCenter, *Behind Closed Doors: Working Conditions of California Household Workers* (Oakland, CA: DataCenter, 2007).

12. Rose Arrieta, "California Domestic Workers Win Long-Sought Bill of Rights," *In These Times*, Sept. 26, 2013.

13. Mark Pazniokas and Keith M. Phaneuf, "Senate's Message for Domestics, 'You Exist, by Law,'" *CT Mirror* (Hartford, CT), May 30, 2015.

Chapter 18

1. Paul Garver, "Massachusetts Legislature Passes Bill to Halt Temp Worker Exploitation," *Talking Union* (blog), Aug. 3, 2012.

2. "Staffing Industry Statistics," American Staffing Association (n.d.), accessed May 25, 2020, https://americanstaffing.net/staffing-research-data/fact-sheets -analysis-staffing-industry-trends/staffing-industry-statistics.

3. The MassCOSH research was complemented by a report from Harris Freeman and George Gonos entitled *The Challenge of Temporary Work in Twenty-First Century Labor Markets: Flexibility with Fairness for the Low-Wage Temporary Workforce* (Amherst: University of Massachusetts, Labor Relations and Research Center, 2011).

4. Reform Employment Agency Law Coalition, "Factsheet on House No. 4076: An Act Establishing a Temporary Worker Right to Know," 2012.

5. As of June 2020, Marcy Goldstein-Gelb was the co-executive director of the National Council for Occupational Safety and Health.

6. We credit the late Lizzie Grossman for her interview with Marcy Goldstein-Gelb for *The Pump Handle* blog in "Day-to-Day Labor: The Hazards of Low-Wage Temping in America," Feb. 9, 2012; and thanks to Kim Krisberg for her reporting and interviews with Tim Bell and Marcela Gallegos for *The Pump Handle* blog in "Temp Workers Organize for Change in an Industry Rife with Reported Abuses," Sept. 12, 2014.

7. Prior to 2015, the Brazilian Worker Center was known as the Brazilian Immigrant Center.

8. Marc Larocque, "OSHA Cites Tribe Mediterranean Foods Following Death of Fall River Man at Taunton Plant," *Taunton Daily Gazette* (Taunton, MA), June 18, 2012.

9. Massachusetts Coalition for Occupational Safety and Health, "Groundbreaking Temp Worker Law Now in Effect!" News Release, Jan. 31, 2013.

10. Ibid.

11. The leadership of the National Staffing Workers Alliance (NSWA) was Tim Bell, of the Chicago Workers' Collaborative; Lou Kimmel, of New Labor; Elvis Mendez, of the Immigrant Worker Center Collaborative; Sheheryar Kaoosji, of the Warehouse Worker Resource Center; and Sean Fulkerson and Mark Meinster, of Warehouse Workers for Justice. NSWA dissolved in 2018.

12. American Public Media's Marketplace and ProPublica, "ProPublica and American Public Media's Marketplace Launch Exclusive Investigation: Taken for a Ride: Temp Agencies and 'Raiteros' in Immigrant America," News Release, Apr. 29, 2018.

13. In 2006, the Illinois law on staffing agencies included a requirement for a temp worker to receive, at the time of dispatch, a Labor Department form that included information such as the nature of the work to be performed; wages offered; terms of transportation; cost of meals or equipment, if any; and contact information for the temp agency and the host employer. Other protections included a paystub with deductions detailed, and wages could not fall below the minimum wage.

14. Rebecca Smith and Claire McKenna, *Temped Out: How the Domestic Outsourcing of Blue-Collar Jobs Harms America's Workers* (New York: National Employment Law Project, 2015), 8.

15. Will Evans, "Kill Bill: How Illinois' Temp Industry Lobbying Quashed Reform," *Reveal*, June 13, 2016; and Will Evans, "When Companies Hire Temp Workers by Race, Black Applicants Lose Out," *Reveal*, Jan. 6, 2016.

16. As of June 2020, Chris Williams was co-director of the National Legal Advocacy Network. Williams had worked closely with state lawmakers in 2006 to pass the Illinois Day and Temporary Labor Services Act.

17. Evans, "Kill Bill."

18. Illinois Legislative Black Caucus Foundation, "Huge Victory for Hundreds of Thousands of Temp Workers," News Release, Mar. 31, 2017.

19. The exact language of the law is "A day and temporary labor service shall attempt to place a current temporary laborer into a permanent position with a client when the client informs the agency of its plan to hire a permanent employee for a position like the positions for which employees are being provided by the agency at the same work location" (Illinois Public Act 100-0517).

20. David Roeder, "'Seal of Approval' Sought to Curb Abuses at Temporary Staffing Firms," *Chicago Sun-Times*, May 26, 2019.

21. Patricia Alex and Kathleen Lynn, "How Port Newark Moves the World," *New Jersey Monthly*, July 18, 2019.

22. George Gonos and Carmen Martino, "Temp Agency Workers in New Jersey's Logistics Hub: The Case for a Union Hiring Hall," *Journal of Labor and Society* 14, no. 4 (2011): 503.

Chapter 19

1. David Cooper and Teresa Kroeger, *Employers Steal Billions from Workers' Paychecks Each Year* (Washington, D.C.: Economic Policy Institute, 2017).

2. Haleigh Svoboda, "Austin Officials Announce Crackdown on Wage Theft," *Texas Tribune*, Nov. 17, 2011.

3. Andrew Schneider, "New Law Tightens Workers Protection Against Stolen Wages," *Houston Public Media*, June 3, 2011.

4. Cynthia S. Hernandez, *Wage Theft in Florida: A Real Problem with Real Solutions* (Research Institute on Social and Economic Policy, Florida International University, 2010); and South Florida Wage Theft Task Force, *Wage Theft in South Florida* (2010), https://risep.fiu.edu/research-publications/workers-rights-econ -justice/wage-theft/2010/wage-theft-stories-in-south-florida/wwwrisep-fiuorg_wp -content_uploads_2010_11_wage-theft-stories.pdf.

5. The worker centers that assisted with the surveys included Wind of the Spirit, Comite de Apoyo a los Trabajadores Agricoles, and Casa Freehold.

6. Immigrants' Rights/International Human Rights Clinic, Center for Social Justice, *All Work and No Pay: Day Laborers, Wage Theft, and Workplace Justice in New Jersey* (Newark, NJ: Seton Hall University School of Law, 2011).

7. Hank Kalet, "Taking a Bigger Bite out of Wage Theft in the Garden State," *NJ Spotlight*, July 17, 2014.

8. Sue Epstein, "New Brunswick Becomes First Town in State to Adopt Ordinance Banning Wage Theft," *NJ.com*, Dec. 31, 2013.

9. Annette Quijano, "We Must Protect Against Workers Losing the Money They're Owed, Assembly Woman Says," *NJ.com*, July 24, 2019.

Chapter 20

1. In July 2019, U.S. Senator Kamala Harris and U.S. Rep. Pramila Jayapal introduced the Domestic Workers Bill of Rights Act (116th Congress, S. 2112 and H.R. 3760).

2. Edna Bonacich and Richard Appelbaum, *Behind the Label: Inequality in the Los Angeles Apparel Industry* (Berkeley: University of California Press, 2000), 293.

3. National Center for Law and Economic Justice et al., *Empty Judgments: The Wage Collection Crisis in New York* (New York, 2015), 5.

The Power Awakened

1. Abby Faulkner, "Pilgrim's Pride Workers Hold Walk-Out over Coronavirus Fears," first broadcast Apr. 29, 2020, by WJON FM 95.3 (St. Cloud, MN).

INDEX

ABOUT THE AUTHORS

Celeste Monforton, director of the Beyond OSHA Project and lecturer at Texas State University, worked in occupational safety for three decades. A sought-after national media commentator, she lives in San Marcos, Texas.

Jane M. Von Bergen, of Philadelphia, is an award-winning journalist who covered labor, the economy, government, and courts for the *Philadelphia Inquirer* for thirty-five years.

PUBLISHING IN THE PUBLIC INTEREST

Thank you for reading this book published by The New Press. The New Press is a nonprofit, public interest publisher. New Press books and authors play a crucial role in sparking conversations about the key political and social issues of our day.

We hope you enjoyed this book and that you will stay in touch with The New Press. Here are a few ways to stay up to date with our books, events, and the issues we cover:

- Sign up at www.thenewpress.com/subscribe to receive updates on New Press authors and issues and to be notified about local events
- Like us on Facebook: www.facebook.com/new pressbooks
- Follow us on Twitter: www.twitter.com/thenew press
- Follow us on Instagram: www.instagram.com/the newpress

Please consider buying New Press books for yourself; for friends and family; or to donate to schools, libraries, community centers, prison libraries, and other organizations involved with the issues our authors write about.

The New Press is a 501(c)(3) nonprofit organization. You can also support our work with a tax-deductible gift by visiting www.thenewpress.com/donate.